THE NATION'S
FAVOURITE
SHAKESPEARE

Also available from BBC Worldwide:

THE NATION'S FAVOURITE POEMS
ISBN: 0 563 38782 3

THE NATION'S FAVOURITE POEMS
(hardback gift edition)
ISBN: 0 563 38487 5

THE NATION'S FAVOURITE LOVE POEMS
ISBN: 0 563 38378 X

THE NATION'S FAVOURITE LOVE POEMS
(hardback gift edition)
ISBN: 0 563 38432 8

THE NATION'S FAVOURITE COMIC POEMS
ISBN: 0 563 38451 4

THE NATION'S FAVOURITE TWENTIETH
CENTURY POEMS
ISBN: 0 563 55143 7

Audio cassettes to accompany the books in this series are produced
by BBC Radio Collection

THE NATION'S FAVOURITE POEMS
ISBN: 0 563 38987 7

THE NATION'S FAVOURITE LOVE POEMS
ISBN: 0 563 38279 1

THE NATION'S FAVOURITE COMIC POEMS
ISBN: 0 563 55850 4

Available from October 1999:

THE NATION'S FAVOURITE SHAKESPEARE
(audio cassette)
ISBN: 0 563 55331 6

The above titles are also available on CD.

THE NATION'S FAVOURITE SHAKESPEARE

— ◇ —

FOREWORD BY

RICHARD BRIERS OBE

Published by
BBC Worldwide Limited,
Woodlands,
80 Wood Lane,
London
W12 0TT

First published 1999

Edited and compiled by Emma Shackleton
Compilation © BBC Worldwide 1999
Extracts taken from The Arden Shakespeare as published by
Thomas Nelson & Sons Ltd, Walton-on-Thames, Surrey.

ISBN 0 563 55142 9

Set in Stempel Garamond by Keystroke,
Jacaranda Lodge, Wolverhampton.
Printed and bound in Great Britain by Martins the Printers Ltd,
Berwick-upon-Tweed.
Cover printed by Belmont Press, Northampton.

CONTENTS

— ◇ —

PLAYS

Comedies

Tragedies

v

Histories

SONNETS

OREWORD BY RICHARD BRIERS OBE

— ◇ —

It is interesting to note, as we approach the Millennium, that Shakespeare's popularity has never been greater. The films of his plays, including Olivier's *Hamlet*, *Richard III* and *Henry V* and Kenneth Branagh's *Much Ado About Nothing* and full-length *Hamlet* have brought the Bard of Avon to a massive world audience.

However, it is vital to have the text before us, to enjoy, study, or simply to marvel at. *The Nation's Favourite Shakespeare* is a perfect accompaniment to the visual treats of the cinema and helps us to understand why the plays and sonnets have survived for over four hundred years and why they will live on as long as our world exists.

These extracts will surely whet the appetite for further explorations into the mind of a man who appears to know everything about human nature. All the great emotions are here: the jealousy of Othello; the ambition of Macbeth; the mental agony of Hamlet; the monumental rage and madness of Lear; the supreme love story of Romeo and Juliet. There is also humour. Those who have never laughed at Malvolio, Bottom or Sir John Falstaff have missed great treats. The person who has not discovered and explored the world of Shakespeare is poor indeed.

'All the world's a stage', and all of us act most of the time. We all have multi-personalities and are capable of profound emotions. It is through reading these plays that we can recognize our inner selves and acquire wisdom that is beyond any classroom.

Of course, being an actor, I am heavily biased. The joy and privilege of actually speaking the language is an exhilarating experience. All actors should have the chance to act in Shakespeare. It stretches voice, body and mind and releases undeveloped potential talent.

When I was training at the Royal Academy of Dramatic Art, I asked our great voice teacher, Clifford Turner, if Shakespeare himself thought his work would survive.

'Of course he did,' Turner replied, with a gentle laugh. 'Read Sonnet 55.'

I hope you will.

PLAYS

Comedies

— ◇ —

THE TAMING OF THE SHREW

Written and first performed 1590–4

Petruchio, a gentleman of Verona, has resolved to marry Katherina, regardless of her wishes and her reputation for shrewish behaviour.

Act II, i (lines 183–95)

PETRUCHIO Good morrow, Kate, for that's your name, I hear.

KATHERINA Well have you heard, but something hard of hearing;
They call me Katherine that do talk of me.

PETRUCHIO You lie, in faith, for you are call'd plain Kate,
And bonny Kate, and sometimes Kate the curst;
But Kate, the prettiest Kate in Christendom,
Kate of Kate Hall, my super-dainty Kate,
For dainties are all Kates, and therefore, Kate,
Take this of me, Kate of my consolation,
Hearing thy mildness prais'd in every town,
Thy virtues spoke of, and thy beauty sounded,
Yet not so deeply as to thee belongs,
Myself am mov'd to woo thee for my wife.

A MIDSUMMER NIGHT'S DREAM

Written and first performed 1594–5

In the woods near Athens the spirit Puck, jester and lieutenant of Oberon, king of the fairies, meets a fairy in the service of Titania, queen of the fairies.

Act II, i (lines 1–57)

PUCK How now, spirit! Whither wander you?
FAIRY   Over hill, over dale,
       Thorough bush, thorough briar,
    Over park, over pale,
       Thorough flood, thorough fire,
    I do wander everywhere,
    Swifter than the moon's sphere;
    And I serve the Fairy Queen,
    To dew her orbs upon the green.
    The cowslips tall her pensioners be,
    In their gold coats spots you see;
    Those be rubies, fairy favours,
    In those freckles live their savours.
    I must go seek some dew-drops here,
    And hang a pearl in every cowslip's ear.
Farewell, thou lob of spirits; I'll be gone;
Our Queen and all her elves come here anon.

PUCK The King doth keep his revels here tonight;
Take heed the Queen come not within his sight;
For Oberon is passing fell and wrath,
Because that she as her attendant hath
A lovely boy, stol'n from an Indian king –
She never had so sweet a changeling;
And jealous Oberon would have the child
Knight of his train, to trace the forests wild:
But she perforce withholds the loved boy,
Crowns him with flowers, and makes him all her joy.

And now they never meet in grove or green,
By fountain clear, or spangled starlight sheen,
But they do square; that all their elves for fear
Creep into acorn-cups, and hide them there.

FAIRY Either I mistake your shape and making quite,
Or else you are that shrewd and knavish sprite
Call'd Robin Goodfellow. Are not you he
That frights the maidens of the villagery,
Skim milk, and sometimes labour in the quern,
And bootless make the breathless housewife churn,
And sometime make the drink to bear no barm,
Mislead night-wanderers, laughing at their harm?
Those that Hobgoblin call you, and sweet Puck,
You do their work, and they shall have good luck.
Are not you he?

PUCK Thou speak'st aright;
I am that merry wanderer of the night.
I jest to Oberon, and make him smile
When I a fat and bean-fed horse beguile,
Neighing in likeness of a filly foal;
And sometime lurk I in a gossip's bowl
In very likeness of a roasted crab,
And when she drinks, against her lips I bob,
And on her wither'd dewlap pour the ale.
The wisest aunt, telling the saddest tale,
Sometime for three-foot stool mistaketh me;
Then slip I from her bum, down topples she,
And 'tailor' cries, and falls into a cough;
And then the whole quire hold their hips and loffe
And waxen in their mirth, and neeze, and swear
A merrier hour was never wasted there.

Oberon and Titania meet. They argue and Titania describes how their quarrel has affected nature and the seasons.

Act II, i (lines 60–117)

OBERON Ill met by moonlight, proud Titania.

TITANIA What, jealous Oberon? Fairies, skip hence;
I have forsworn his bed and company.

OBERON Tarry, rash wanton; am not I thy lord?

TITANIA Then I must be thy lady; but I know
When thou hast stol'n away from fairy land,
And in the shape of Corin, sat all day
Playing on pipes of corn, and versing love
To amorous Phillida. Why art thou here,
Come from the farthest step of India,
But that, forsooth, the bouncing Amazon,
Your buskin'd mistress and your warrior love,
To Theseus must be wedded, and you come
To give their bed joy and prosperity?

OBERON How canst thou thus, for shame, Titania,
Glance at my credit with Hippolyta,
Knowing I know thy love to Theseus?
Didst not thou lead him through the glimmering night
From Perigouna, whom he ravished;
And make him with fair Aegles break his faith,
With Ariadne and Antiopa?

TITANIA These are the forgeries of jealousy:
And never, since the middle summer's spring,
Met we on hill, in dale, forest or mead,
By paved fountain, or by rushy brook,
Or in the beached margent of the sea,
To dance our ringlets to the whistling wind,
But with thy brawls thou has disturb'd our sport.
Therefore the winds, piping to us in vain,
As in revenge have suck'd up from the sea

8

Contagious fogs; which, falling in the land,
Hath every pelting river made so proud
That they have overborne their continents.
The ox hath therefore stretch'd his yoke in vain,
The ploughman lost his sweat, and the green corn
Hath rotted ere his youth attain'd a beard;
The fold stands empty in the drowned field,
And crows are fatted with the murrion flock;
The nine-men's-morris is fill'd up with mud,
And the quaint mazes in the wanton green
For lack of tread are undistinguishable.
The human mortals want their winter cheer:
No night is now with hymn or carol blest.
Therefore the moon, the governess of floods,
Pale in her anger, washes all the air,
That rheumatic diseases do abound.
And thorough this distemperature we see
The seasons alter: hoary-headed frosts
Fall in the fresh lap of the crimson rose;
And on old Hiems' thin and icy crown,
An odorous chaplet of sweet summer buds
Is, as in mockery, set; the spring, the summer,
The childing autumn, angry winter, change
Their wonted liveries; and the mazed world,
By their increase, now knows not which is which.
And this same progeny of evils comes
From our debate, from our dissension;
We are their parents and original.

Oberon tells Puck to go and find the herb called 'love-in-idleness'.

Act II, i (lines 149–76)

OBERON My gentle Puck, come hither. Thou rememb'rest
Since once I sat upon a promontory,
And heard a mermaid on a dolphin's back
Uttering such dulcet and harmonious breath
That the rude sea grew civil at her song
And certain stars shot madly from their spheres
To hear the sea-maid's music?

PUCK I remember.

OBERON That very time I saw (but thou couldst not),
Flying between the cold moon and the earth,
Cupid all arm'd: a certain aim he took
At a fair vestal, throned by the west,
And loos'd his love-shaft smartly from his bow
As it should pierce a hundred thousand hearts.
But I might see young Cupid's fiery shaft
Quench'd in the chaste beams of the watery moon;
And the imperial votress passed on,
In maiden meditation, fancy-free.
Yet mark'd I where the bolt of Cupid fell:
It fell upon a little western flower,
Before milk-white, now purple with love's wound:
And maidens call it 'love-in-idleness'.
Fetch me that flower; the herb I show'd thee once.
The juice of it, on sleeping eyelids laid,
Will make or man or woman madly dote
Upon the next live creature that it sees.
Fetch me this herb, and be thou here again
Ere the leviathan can swim a league.

PUCK I'll put a girdle round about the earth
In forty minutes.

When Puck returns with the herb, Oberon tells him to anoint the eyes of Titania with it. Having taken pity on Helena, who is in love with Demetrius, he also tells Puck to anoint Demetrius's eyes.

Act II, i (lines 247–68)

OBERON Hast thou the flower there? Welcome, wanderer.

PUCK Ay, there it is.

OBERON I pray thee give it me.
I know a bank where the wild thyme blows,
Where oxlips and the nodding violet grows,
Quite over-canopied with luscious woodbine,
With sweet musk-roses, and with eglantine.
There sleeps Titania sometime of the night,
Lull'd in these flowers with dances and delight;
And there the snake throws her enamell'd skin,
Weed wide enough to wrap a fairy in;
And with the juice of this I'll streak her eyes,
And make her full of hateful fantasies.
Take thou some of it, and seek through this grove:
A sweet Athenian lady is in love
With a disdainful youth; anoint his eyes;
But do it when the next thing he espies
May be the lady. Thou shalt know the man
By the Athenian garments he hath on.
Effect it with some care, that he may prove
More fond on her than she upon her love:
And look thou meet me ere the first cock crow.

PUCK Fear not, my lord, your servant shall do so.

Peter Quince, Nick Bottom, Snug, Francis Flute, Tom Snout and Robin Starveling, craftsmen of Athens, have come to the woods to rehearse a scene from the story of Pyramus and Thisbe for the wedding celebrations of Theseus, Duke of Athens, and Hippolyta, Queen of the Amazons.

Act III, i (lines 1–33)

BOTTOM Are we all met?

QUINCE Pat, pat; and here's a marvellous convenient place for our rehearsal. This green plot shall be our stage, this hawthorn-brake our tiring-house; and we will do it in action, as we will do it before the Duke.

BOTTOM Peter Quince!

QUINCE What sayest thou, bully Bottom?

BOTTOM There are things in this comedy of Pyramus and Thisbe that will never please. First, Pyramus must draw a sword to kill himself; which the ladies cannot abide. How answer you that?

SNOUT Byrlakin, a parlous fear.

STARVELING I believe we must leave the killing out, when all is done.

BOTTOM Not a whit; I have a device to make all well. Write me a prologue, and let the prologue seem to say we will do no harm with our swords, and that Pyramus is not killed indeed; and for the more better assurance, tell them that I, Pyramus, am not Pyramus, but Bottom the weaver. This will put them out of fear.

QUINCE Well, we will have such a prologue; and it shall be written in eight and six.

BOTTOM No, make it two more; let it be written in eight and eight.

SNOUT Will not the ladies be afeared of the lion?

STARVELING I fear it, I promise you.

BOTTOM Masters, you ought to consider with yourself; to bring in (God shield us!) a lion among ladies is a most dreadful thing; for there is not a more fearful wild-fowl than your lion living; and we ought to look to't.

SNOUT Therefore another prologue must tell he is not a lion.

Puck has anointed the eyes of Lysander, whom he has mistaken for Demetrius. As a result Lysander has fallen in love with Helena. Hermia is distraught at the change in Lysander, and Helena believes that Hermia has conspired with Lysander and Demetrius against her. The two women quarrel.

Act III, ii (lines 282–98)

HERMIA O me!
[*to Helena*] You juggler! You canker-blossom!
You thief of love! What, have you come by night
And stol'n my love's heart from him?

HELENA Fine, i'faith!
Have you no modesty, no maiden shame,
No touch of bashfulness? What, will you tear
Impatient answers from my gentle tongue?
Fie, fie, you counterfeit! You puppet you!

HERMIA 'Puppet'! Why, so? Ay, that way goes the game!
Now I perceive that she hath made compare
Between our statures; she hath urg'd her height;
And with her personage, her tall personage,
Her height, forsooth, she hath prevail'd with him.
And are you grown so high in his esteem
Because I am so dwarfish and so low?
How low am I, thou painted maypole? Speak:
How low am I? I am not yet so low
But that my nails can reach unto thine eyes.

*Hermia, Helena, Lysander and Demetrius have told Theseus
and Hippolyta of their strange experiences in the woods.
Theseus and Hippolyta discuss their tale.*

Act V, i (lines 1–22)

HIPPOLYTA 'Tis strange, my Theseus, that these lovers speak of.

THESEUS More strange than true. I never may believe
These antique fables, nor these fairy toys.
Lovers and madmen have such seething brains,
Such shaping fantasies, that apprehend
More than cool reason ever comprehends.
The lunatic, the lover, and the poet
Are of imagination all compact:
One sees more devils than vast hell can hold;
That is the madman: the lover, all as frantic,
Sees Helen's beauty in a brow of Egypt:
The poet's eye, in a fine frenzy rolling,
Doth glance from heaven to earth, from earth to heaven;
And as imagination bodies forth
The forms of things unknown, the poet's pen
Turns them to shapes, and gives to airy nothing
A local habitation and a name.
Such tricks hath strong imagination,
That if it would but apprehend some joy,
It comprehends some bringer of that joy:
Or, in the night, imagining some fear,
How easy is a bush suppos'd a bear!

As the wedding party disperses Puck, Oberon and Titania appear to give their blessing to the married couples and to conclude the play.

Act V, i (lines 365–432)

PUCK   Now the hungry lion roars,
And the wolf behowls the moon;
Whilst the heavy ploughman snores,
All with weary task fordone.
Now the wasted brands do glow,
Whilst the screech-owl, screeching loud,
Puts the wretch that lies in woe
In remembrance of a shroud.
Now it is the time of night
That the graves, all gaping wide,
Every one lets forth his sprite
In the church-way paths to glide.
And we fairies, that do run
By the triple Hecate's team
From the presence of the sun,
Following darkness like a dream,
Now are frolic; not a mouse
Shall disturb this hallow'd house.
I am sent with broom before
To sweep the dust behind the door.

Enter OBERON *and* TITANIA, *the King and Queen of Fairies, with all their train.*

OBERON   Through the house give glimmering light
By the dead and drowsy fire;
Every elf and fairy sprite
Hop as light as bird from briar;
And this ditty after me
Sing, and dance it trippingly.

TITANIA   First rehearse your song by rote,
To each word a warbling note;
Hand in hand, with fairy grace,
Will we sing, and bless this place.

[*Oberon leading, the Fairies sing and dance.*]

OBERON   Now, until the break of day,
          Through this house each fairy stray.
          To the best bride-bed will we,
          Which by us shall blessed be;
          And the issue there create
          Ever shall be fortunate.
          So shall all the couples three
          Ever true in loving be;
          And the blots of Nature's hand
          Shall not in their issue stand:
          Never mole, hare-lip, nor scar,
          Nor mark prodigious, such as are
          Despised in nativity,
          Shall upon their children be.
          With this field-dew consecrate,
          Every fairy take his gait,
          And each several chamber bless
          Through this palace with sweet peace;
          And the owner of it blest,
          Ever shall in safety rest.
          Trip away; make no stay;
          Meet me all by break of day.

                                        Exeunt all but Puck.

PUCK [*to the audience*]
          If we shadows have offended,
          Think but this, and all is mended,
          That you have but slumber'd here
          While these visions did appear.
          And this weak and idle theme,
          No more yielding but a dream,
          Gentles, do not reprehend:
          If you pardon, we will mend.
          And, as I am an honest Puck,
          If we have unearned luck
          Now to 'scape the serpent's tongue,
          We will make amends ere long;
          Else the Puck a liar call.
          So, goodnight unto you all.
          Give me your hands, if we be friends,
          And Robin shall restore amends.   *Exit.*

THE MERCHANT OF VENICE

Written and first performed 1596–7

The merchant Antonio acknowledges his sadness to his friends
Salerio and Solanio who speculate on its causes.

Act I, i (lines 1–40)

ANTONIO In sooth I know not why I am so sad,
It wearies me, you say it wearies you;
But how I caught it, found it, or came by it,
What stuff 'tis made of, whereof it is born,
I am to learn:
And such a want-wit sadness makes of me,
That I have much ado to know myself.

SALERIO Your mind is tossing on the ocean,
There where your argosies with portly sail
Like signiors and rich burghers on the flood,
Or as it were the pageants of the sea,
Do overpeer the petty traffickers
That cur'sy to them (do them reverence)
As they fly by them with their woven wings.

SOLANIO Believe me sir, had I such venture forth,
The better part of my affections would
Be with my hopes abroad. I should be still
Plucking the grass to know where sits the wind,
Piring in maps for ports, and piers and roads:
And every object that might make me fear
Misfortune to my ventures, out of doubt
Would make me sad.

SALERIO My wind cooling my broth,
Would blow me to an ague when I thought
What harm a wind too great might do at sea.
I should not see the sandy hour-glass run
But I should think of shallows and of flats,

18

And see my wealthy Andrew dock'd in sand
Vailing her high top lower than her ribs
To kiss her burial; should I go to church
And see the holy edifice of stone
And not bethink me straight of dangerous rocks,
Which touching but my gentle vessel's side
Would scatter all her spices on the stream,
Enrobe the roaring waters with my silks,
And in a word, but even now worth this,
And now worth nothing? Shall I have the thought
To think on this, and shall I lack the thought
That such a thing bechanc'd would make me sad?
But tell not me, I know Antonio
Is sad to think upon his merchandise.

Antonio asks Shylock to lend him money to pay for Bassanio's journey to woo Portia at Belmont. Shylock challenges Antonio over his behaviour towards him.

Act I, iii (lines 104–27)

SHYLOCK Signior Antonio, many a time and oft
In the Rialto you have rated me
About my moneys and my usances:
Still have I borne it with a patient shrug,
(For suff'rance is the badge of all our tribe)
You call me misbeliever, cut-throat dog,
And spet upon my Jewish gaberdine,
And all for use of that which is mine own.
Well then, it now appears you need my help:
Go to then, you come to me, and you say,
'Shylock, we would have moneys,' you say so:
You that did void your rheum upon my beard,
And foot me as you spurn a stranger cur
Over your threshold, moneys is your suit.
What should I say to you? Should I not say
'Hath a dog money? is it possible
A cur can lend three thousand ducats?' or
Shall I bend low, and in a bondman's key
With bated breath, and whisp'ring humbleness
Say this:
'Fair sir, you spet on me on Wednesday last,
You spurn'd me such a day, another time
You call'd me dog: and for these courtesies
I'll lend you thus much moneys'?

Shylock has lent Antonio money in return for a pound of Antonio's flesh if he forfeits the loan. With the news that one of Antonio's ships is lost at sea, Shylock swears that he will take the pound of flesh if Antonio fails to meet his bond.

Act III, i (lines 47–67)

SALERIO Why I am sure if he forfeit, thou wilt not take his flesh, – what's that good for?

SHYLOCK To bait fish withal, – if it will feed nothing else, it will feed my revenge; he hath disgrac'd me, and hind'red me half a million, laugh'd at my losses, mock'd at my gains, scorned my nation, thwarted my bargains, cooled my friends, heated mine enemies, – and what's his reason? I am a Jew. Hath not a Jew eyes? hath not a Jew hands, organs, dimensions, senses, affections, passions? fed with the same food, hurt with the same weapons, subject to the same diseases, healed by the same means, warmed and cooled by the same winter and summer as a Christian is? – if you prick us do we not bleed? if you tickle us do we not laugh? If you poison us do we not die? and if you wrong us shall we not revenge – if we are like you in the rest, we will resemble you in that. If a Jew wrong a Christian, what is his humility? revenge! If a Christian wrong a Jew, what should his sufferance be by Christian example? – why revenge! The villainy you teach me I will execute, and it shall go hard but I will better the instruction.

Portia is now betrothed to Bassanio and has secretly followed him from Belmont to Venice. Disguised as a lawyer named Balthazar, she argues that mercy should be shown, but Shylock demands his bond.

Act IV, i (lines 180–205)

PORTIA Then must the Jew be merciful.

SHYLOCK On what compulsion must I? tell me that.

PORTIA The quality of mercy is not strain'd,
It droppeth as the gentle rain from heaven
Upon the place beneath: it is twice blest,
It blesseth him that gives, and him that takes,
'Tis mightiest in the mightiest, it becomes
The throned monarch better than his crown.
His sceptre shows the force of temporal power,
The attribute to awe and majesty,
Wherein doth sit the dread and fear of kings:
But mercy is above this sceptred sway,
It is enthroned in the hearts of kings,
It is an attribute to God himself;
And earthly power doth then show likest God's
When mercy seasons justice: therefore Jew,
Though justice be thy plea, consider this,
That in the course of justice, none of us
Should see salvation: we do pray for mercy,
And that same prayer doth teach us all to render
The deeds of mercy. I have spoke thus much
To mitigate the justice of thy plea,
Which if thou follow, this strict court of Venice
Must needs give sentence 'gainst the merchant there.

SHYLOCK My deeds upon my head! I crave the law,
The penalty and forfeit of my bond.

Jessica, Shylock's daughter, and Lorenzo, who have eloped from Venice, are staying at Portia's home at Belmont.

Act V, i (lines 1–24)

LORENZO The moon shines bright. In such a night as this,
When the sweet wind did gently kiss the trees,
And they did make no noise, in such a night
Troilus methinks mounted the Trojan walls,
And sigh'd his soul toward the Grecian tents
Where Cressid lay that night.

JESSICA In such a night
Did Thisbe fearfully o'ertrip the dew,
And saw the lion's shadow ere himself,
And ran dismayed away.

LORENZO In such a night
Stood Dido with a willow in her hand
Upon the wild sea banks, and waft her love
To come again to Carthage.

JESSICA In such a night
Medea gathered the enchanted herbs
That did renew old Aeson.

LORENZO In such a night
Did Jessica steal from the wealthy Jew,
And with an unthrift love did run from Venice,
As far as Belmont.

JESSICA In such a night
Did young Lorenzo swear he loved her well,
Stealing her soul with many vows of faith,
And ne'er a true one.

LORENZO In such a night
Did pretty Jessica (like a little shrew)
Slander her love, and he forgave it her.

JESSICA I would out-night you did nobody come:
But hark, I hear the footing of a man.

As Jessica and Lorenzo wait for Portia and Nerissa to arrive from Venice, they discuss the power of music.

Act V, i (lines 54–88)

LORENZO How sweet the moonlight sleeps upon this bank!
Here will we sit, and let the sounds of music
Creep in our ears – soft stillness and the night
Become the touches of sweet harmony:
Sit Jessica, – look how the floor of heaven
Is thick inlaid with patens of bright gold,
There's not the smallest orb which thou behold'st
But in his motion like an angel sings,
Still quiring to the young-ey'd cherubins;
Such harmony is in immortal souls,
But whilst this muddy vesture of decay
Doth grossly close it in, we cannot hear it:

Enter musicians.

Come ho! and wake Diana with a hymn,
With sweetest touches pierce your mistress' ear,
And draw her home with music.   [*Music.*]

JESSICA I am never merry when I hear sweet music.

LORENZO The reason is your spirits are attentive:
For do but note a wild and wanton herd
Or race of youthful and unhandled colts
Fetching mad bounds, bellowing and neighing loud,
Which is the hot condition of their blood, –
If they but hear perchance a trumpet sound,
Or any air of music touch their ears,
You shall perceive them make a mutual stand,
Their savage eyes turn'd to a modest gaze,
By the sweet power of music: therefore the poet
Did feign that Orpheus drew trees, stones, and floods,
Since naught so stockish, hard, and full of rage,

But music for the time doth change his nature, –
The man that hath no music in himself,
Nor is not moved with concord of sweet sounds,
Is fit for treasons, stratagems, and spoils,
The motions of his spirit are dull as night,
And his affections dark as Erebus:
Let no such man be trusted: – mark the music.

Written and first performed 1598–9

Don Pedro, Prince of Aragon, has arranged the marriage of Hero, the daughter of Leonato, the governor of Messina, to Lord Claudio. Now he banters with Beatrice, Hero's cousin.

Act II, i (lines 294–317)

DON PEDRO In faith, lady, you have a merry heart.

BEATRICE Yea, my lord, I thank it, poor fool, it keeps on the windy side of care. My cousin tells him in his ear that he is in her heart.

CLAUDIO And so she doth, cousin.

BEATRICE Good Lord, for alliance! Thus goes everyone to the world but I, and I am sunburnt. I may sit in a corner and cry 'Heigh-ho for a husband!'

DON PEDRO Lady Beatrice, I will get you one.

BEATRICE I would rather have one of your father's getting. Hath your Grace ne'er a brother like you? Your father got excellent husbands, if a maid could come by them.

DON PEDRO Will you have me, lady?

BEATRICE No, my lord, unless I might have another for working days: your Grace is too costly to wear every day. But I beseech your Grace pardon me, I was born to speak all mirth and no matter.

DON PEDRO Your silence most offends me, and to be merry best becomes you, for out o' question, you were born in a merry hour.

BEATRICE No, sure, my lord, my mother cried, but then there was a star danced, and under that was I born. Cousins, God give you joy!

Benedick has been duped by his friends into believing that Beatrice loves him. He decides to reciprocate her feelings.

Act II, iii (lines 212–35)

BENEDICK [*coming forward*] This can be no trick: the conference was sadly borne; they have the truth of this from Hero. They seem to pity the lady: it seems her affections have their full bent. Love me? Why, it must be requited. I hear how I am censured: they say I will bear myself proudly, if I perceive the love come from her; they say too that she will rather die than give any sign of affection. I did never think to marry: I must not seem proud: happy are they that hear their detractions and can put them to mending. They say the lady is fair – 'tis a truth, I can bear them witness; and virtuous – 'tis so, I cannot reprove it; and wise, but for loving me – by my troth, it is no addition to her wit, nor no great argument of her folly, for I will be horribly in love with her. I may chance have some odd quirks and remnants of wit broken on me because I have railed so long against marriage: but doth not the appetite alter? A man loves the meat in his youth that he cannot endure in his age. Shall quips and sentences and these paper bullets of the brain awe a man from the career of his humour? No, the world must be peopled. When I said I would die a bachelor, I did not think I should live till I were married. Here comes Beatrice. By this day, she's a fair lady! I do spy some marks of love in her.

Claudio has been tricked by Borachio and Conrad, two followers of Don Pedro's brother, Don John, into believing that Hero is unfaithful. On their wedding day he accuses her of falsehood. When Benedick later declares his love for Beatrice, Beatrice challenges him to kill Claudio, his friend, for slandering Hero.

Act IV, i (lines 266–305)

BENEDICK I do love nothing in the world so well as you – is not that strange?

BEATRICE As strange as the thing I know not. It were as possible for me to say I loved nothing so well as you, but believe me not; and yet I lie not; I confess nothing, nor I deny nothing. I am sorry for my cousin.

BENEDICK By my sword, Beatrice, thou lovest me.

BEATRICE Do not swear and eat it.

BENEDICK I will swear by it that you love me, and I will make him eat it that says I love not you.

BEATRICE Will you not eat your word?

BENEDICK With no sauce that can be devised to it. I protest I love thee.

BEATRICE Why then, God forgive me!

BENEDICK What offence, sweet Beatrice?

BEATRICE You have stayed me in a happy hour, I was about to protest I loved you.

BENEDICK And do it with all thy heart.

BEATRICE I love you with so much of my heart that none is left to protest.

BENEDICK Come, bid me do anything for thee.

BEATRICE Kill Claudio!

BENEDICK Ha, not for the wide world!

BEATRICE You kill me to deny it. Farewell.

BENEDICK Tarry, sweet Beatrice.

BEATRICE I am gone, though I am here; there is no love in you; nay I pray you let me go.

BENEDICK Beatrice –

BEATRICE In faith, I will go.

BENEDICK We'll be friends first.

BEATRICE You dare easier be friends with me than fight with mine enemy.

BENEDICK Is Claudio thine enemy?

BEATRICE Is a not approved in the height a villain, that hath slandered, scorned, dishonoured my kinswoman? O that I were a man! What, bear her in hand until they come to take hands, and then with public accusation, uncovered slander, unmitigated rancour – O God that I were a man! I would eat his heart in the market-place.

Borachio and Conrade have been apprehended and appear before Dogberry, the master constable.

Act IV, ii (lines 72–85)

CONRADE Away! You are an ass, you are an ass.

DOGBERRY Dost thou not suspect my place? Dost thou not suspect my years? O that he were here to write me down an ass! But masters, remember that I am an ass: though it be not written down, yet forget not that I am an ass. No, thou villain, thou art full of piety, as shall be proved upon thee by good witness. I am a wise fellow, and which is more, an officer, and which is more, a householder, and which is more, as pretty a piece of flesh as any is in Messina, and one that knows the law, go to, and a rich fellow enough, go to, and a fellow that hath had losses, and one that hath two gowns, and everything handsome about him. Bring him away! O that I had been writ down an ass!

AS YOU LIKE IT

Written and first performed about 1599

Jaques is an attendant of Duke Senior, who was banished when his dukedom was usurped by his brother Duke Frederick. Duke Senior and his entourage are living in the Forest of Arden. Here, Jacques tells the Duke of his encounter with Touchstone, Duke Frederick's court jester, who has fled with the Duke's daughters, Rosalind and Celia, into the Forest of Arden.

Act II, vii (lines 12–34)

JAQUES   A fool, a fool! I met a fool i'th' forest,
A motley fool: a miserable world!
As I do live by food, I met a fool,
Who laid him down and bask'd him in the sun,
And rail'd on Lady Fortune in good terms,
In good set terms, and yet a motley fool.
'Good morrow, fool,' quoth I. 'No, sir,' quoth he,
'Call me not fool, till heaven hath sent me fortune.'
And then he drew a dial from his poke,
And looking on it, with lack-lustre eye,
Says, very wisely, 'It is ten o'clock.
Thus we may see,' quoth he, 'how the world wags:
'Tis but an hour ago since it was nine,
And after one hour more 'twill be eleven;
And so from hour to hour, we ripe, and ripe,
And then from hour to hour, we rot, and rot,
And thereby hangs a tale'. When I did hear
The motley fool thus moral on the time,
My lungs began to crow like chanticleer,
That fools should be so deep-contemplative;
And I did laugh, sans intermission,
An hour by his dial. O noble fool!
A worthy fool! Motley's the only wear.

Orlando, the second son of the deceased Sir Roland de Boys, has also fled to the Forest of Arden with his father's elderly servant Adam after hearing that his elder brother Oliver intends to have him murdered. In the forest he surprises the party of Duke Senior to demand food for Adam, but then finds he is among friends.

Act II, vii (lines 106–19)

ORLANDO Pardon me, I pray you.
I thought that all things had been savage here,
And therefore put I on the countenance
Of stern commandment. But whate'er you are
That in this desert inaccessible
Under the shade of melancholy boughs,
Lose and neglect the creeping hours of time;
If ever you have look'd on better days;
If ever been where bells have knoll'd to church;
If ever sat at any good man's feast;
If ever from your eyelids wip'd a tear,
And know what 'tis to pity and be pitied,
Let gentleness my strong enforcement be;
In the which hope, I blush, and hide my sword.

As Orlando goes to fetch Adam, Jaques muses upon the seven ages of man.

Act II, vii (lines 139–64)

JAQUES All the world's a stage,
And all the men and women merely players.
They have their exits and their entrances,
And one man in his time plays many parts,
His acts being seven ages. At first the infant,
Mewling and puking in the nurse's arms.
Then, the whining school-boy with his satchel
And shining morning face, creeping like snail
Unwillingly to school. And then the lover,
Sighing like furnace, with a woeful ballad
Made to his mistress' eyebrow. Then, a soldier,
Full of strange oaths, and bearded like the pard,
Jealous in honour, sudden, and quick in quarrel,
Seeking the bubble reputation
Even in the cannon's mouth. And then, the justice,
In fair round belly, with good capon lin'd,
With eyes severe, and beard of formal cut,
Full of wise saws, and modern instances,
And so he plays his part. The sixth age shifts
Into the lean and slipper'd pantaloon,
With spectacles on nose, and pouch on side,
His youthful hose well sav'd, a world too wide
For his shrunk shank, and his big manly voice,
Turning again toward childish treble, pipes
And whistles in his sound. Last scene of all,
That ends this strange eventful history,
Is second childishness and mere oblivion,
Sans teeth, sans eyes, sans taste, sans everything.

Having promised to marry Audrey the goat herd, Touchstone has secretly arranged a false wedding ceremony.

Act III, iii (lines 1–38)

TOUCHSTONE Come apace good Audrey. I will fetch up your goats, Audrey. And how Audrey, am I the man yet? Doth my simple feature content you?

AUDREY Your features? Lord warrant us! What features?

TOUCHSTONE I am here with thee and thy goats, as the most capricious poet, honest Ovid, was among the Goths.

JAQUES [*aside*] O knowledge ill-inhabited, worse than Jove in a thatched house!

TOUCHSTONE When a man's verses cannot be understood, nor a man's good wit seconded with the forward child, under-standing, it strikes a man more dead than a great reckoning in a little room. Truly, I would the gods had made thee poetical.

AUDREY I do not know what 'poetical' is. Is it honest in deed and word? Is it a true thing?

TOUCHSTONE No truly; for the truest poetry is the most feigning, and lovers are given to poetry; and what they swear in poetry may be said as lovers they do feign.

AUDREY Do you wish then that the gods had made me poetical?

TOUCHSTONE I do truly. For thou swear'st to me thou art honest. Now if thou wert a poet, I might have some hope thou didst feign.

AUDREY Would you not have me honest?

TOUCHSTONE No truly, unless thou wert hard-favoured; for honesty coupled to beauty is to have honey a sauce to sugar.

JAQUES [*aside*] A material fool!

AUDREY Well, I am not fair, and therefore I pray the gods make me honest.

TOUCHSTONE Truly, and to cast away honesty upon a foul slut were to put good meat into an unclean dish.

AUDREY I am not a slut, though I thank the gods I am foul.

TOUCHSTONE Well, praised be the gods for thy foulness; sluttishness may come hereafter.

Orlando is in love with Rosalind, whom he has met in the court of Duke Frederick. In the Forest Rosalind is in disguise as a young man named Ganymede. When Orlando and Rosalind as Ganymede first met in the Forest she offered to cure him of his love if he imagined her to be Rosalind. Here, she rejects his claim that he will die if Rosalind will not love him.

Act IV, i (lines 89–102)

ROSALIND The poor world is almost six thousand years old, and in all this time there was not any man died in his own person, videlicet, in a love-cause. Troilus had his brains dashed out with a Grecian club, yet he did what he could to die before, and he is one of the patterns of love. Leander, he would have lived many a fair year though Hero had turned nun, if it had not been for a hot mid summer night; for, good youth, he went but forth to wash him in the Hellespont, and being taken with the cramp, was drowned, and the foolish chroniclers of that age found it was Hero of Sestos. But these are all lies: men have died from time to time and worms have eaten them, but not for love.

TWELFTH NIGHT

....

Written in 1601 and first performed in 1602

Orsino, Duke of Illyria, reflects on his love for a noble woman, Olivia.

Act I, i (lines 1–15)

ORSINO If music be the food of love, play on,
Give me excess of it, that, surfeiting,
The appetite may sicken, and so die.
That strain again, it had a dying fall:
O, it came o'er my ear like the sweet sound
That breathes upon a bank of violets,
Stealing and giving odour. Enough, no more;
'Tis not so sweet now as it was before.
O spirit of love, how quick and fresh art thou,
That notwithstanding thy capacity
Receiveth as the sea, nought enters there,
Of what validity and pitch soe'er,
But falls into abatement and low price,
Even in a minute! So full of shapes is fancy,
That it alone is high fantastical.

Viola has been separated from her brother Sebastian since their ship foundered at sea. She has arrived in Illyria and, disguised as a young man, has found employment with Orsino, with whom she has fallen in love. Orsino has sent her to woo Olivia on his behalf, but Olivia has fallen in love with the disguised Viola. Here, Orsino and Viola discuss Olivia's response to Orsino's courtship.

Act II, iv (lines 90–123)

VIOLA Say that some lady, as perhaps there is,
Hath for your love as great a pang of heart
As you have for Olivia: you cannot love her:
You tell her so. Must she not then be answer'd?

ORSINO There is no woman's sides
Can bide the beating of so strong a passion
As love doth give my heart; no woman's heart
So big, to hold so much: they lack retention.
Alas, their love may be call'd appetite,
No motion of the liver, but the palate,
That suffers surfeit, cloyment, and revolt;
But mine is all as hungry as the sea,
And can digest as much. Make no compare
Between that love a woman can bear me
And that I owe Olivia.

VIOLA Ay, but I know –

ORSINO What dost thou know?

VIOLA Too well what love women to men may owe:
In faith, they are as true of heart as we.
My father had a daughter lov'd a man,
As it might be perhaps, were I a woman,
I should your lordship.

ORSINO And what's her history?

VIOLA A blank, my lord: she never told her love,
But let concealment like a worm i'th' bud
Feed on her damask cheek: she pin'd in thought,

And with a green and yellow melancholy
She sat like Patience on a monument,
Smiling at grief. Was not this love indeed?
We men may say more, swear more, but indeed
Our shows are more than will: for still we prove
Much in our vows, but little in our love.

ORSINO But died thy sister of her love, my boy?

VIOLA I am all the daughters of my father's house,
And all the brothers too: and yet I know not.
Sir, shall I to this lady?

THE WINTER'S TALE

Written and first performed 1609–10

Leontes, King of Sicilia, and Polixenes, King of Bohemia, have been friends since childhood. Leontes has asked his wife, Hermione, to urge Polixenes to extend his stay in Sicilia before returning home. She succeeds, but as the banter between Hermione and Polixenes continues Leontes becomes overwhelmingly jealous.

Act I, ii (lines 185–207)

LEONTES Gone already!
Inch-thick, knee-deep; o'er head and ears a fork'd one.
Go, play, boy, play: thy mother plays, and I
Play too; but so disgrac'd a part, whose issue
Will hiss me to my grave: contempt and clamour
Will be my knell. Go, play, boy, play. There have been,
(Or I am much deceiv'd) cuckolds ere now,
And many a man there is (even at this present,
Now, while I speak this) holds his wife by th' arm,
That little thinks she has been sluic'd in's absence
And his pond fish'd by his next neighbour, by
Sir Smile, his neighbour: nay, there's comfort in't,
Whiles other men have gates, and those gates open'd,
As mine, against their will. Should all despair
That have revolted wives, the tenth of mankind
Would hang themselves. Physic for't there's none;
It is a bawdy planet, that will strike
Where 'tis predominant; and 'tis powerful, think it,
From east, west, north, and south; be it concluded,
No barricado for a belly. Know't,
It will let in and out the enemy,
With bag and baggage: many thousand on's
Have the disease, and feel't not. How now, boy?

Leontes has ordered Camillo to kill Polixenes, but instead Camillo has told Polixenes of his danger and has fled with him. Leontes takes this as another sign of Hermione's and Polixenes's treachery.

Act II, i (lines 36–52)

LEONTES How blest am I
In my just censure! in my true opinion!
Alack, for lesser knowledge! how accurs'd
In being so blest! There may be in the cup
A spider steep'd, and one may drink, depart,
And yet partake no venom (for his knowledge
Is not infected); but if one present
Th'abhorr'd ingredient to his eye, make known
How he hath drunk, he cracks his gorge, his sides,
With violent hefts. I have drunk, and seen the spider.
Camillo was his help in this, his pandar:
There is a plot against my life, my crown;
All's true that is mistrusted: that false villain,
Whom I employ'd, was pre-employ'd by him:
He has discover'd my design, and I
Remain a pinch'd thing; yea, a very trick
For them to play at will.

Sixteen years have passed since Hermione gave birth to a daughter while imprisoned by Leontes. Leontes ordered that the baby be abandoned in a foreign country and she has been reared by an aged shepherd in Bohemia. Named Perdita to describe her fate, she is unaware of her origins. The shepherd has a son, the clown, whom the thief Autolycus comes across when looking for dupes near Perdita's home.

Act IV, iii (lines 1–35)

Enter AUTOLYCUS, *singing.*

When daffodils begin to peer,
    With heigh! the doxy over the dale,
Why then comes in the sweet o'the year,
    For the red blood reigns in the winter's pale.

The white sheet bleaching on the hedge,
    With hey! the sweet birds, O how they sing!
Doth set my pugging tooth an edge;
    For a quart of ale is a dish for a king.

The lark, that tirra-lirra chants,
    With heigh! with heigh! the thrush and the jay,
Are summer songs for me and my aunts,
    While we lie tumbling in the hay.

I have served Prince Florizel, and in my time wore three-pile, but now I am out of service.

But shall I go mourn for that, my dear?
    The pale moon shines by night:
And when I wander here and there,
    I then do most go right.

If tinkers may have leave to live,
    And bear the sow-skin budget,
Then my account I well may give,
    And in the stocks avouch it.

My traffic is sheets; when the kite builds, look to lesser linen. My father named me Autolycus; who, being as I am, littered under Mercury, was likewise a snapper-up of unconsidered trifles. With die and drab I purchased this caparison, and my revenue is the silly cheat. Gallows and knock are too powerful on the highway: beating and hanging are terrors to me: for the life to come, I sleep out the thought of it. A prize! a prize!

Enter CLOWN.

CLOWN Let me see: every 'leven wether tods; every tod yields pound and odd shilling: fifteen hundred shorn, what comes the wool to?

AUTOLYCUS [*aside*] If the springe hold, the cock's mine.

Perdita is the hostess at the shepherd's sheep-shearing party.
Florizel, the son of Polixenes, has come to the party to court Perdita.
He has been followed there by his father and Camillo, who are
both disguised. The shepherd encourages the shy Perdita
to entertain the guests.

Act IV, iv (lines 55–136)

SHEPHERD Fie, daughter! when my old wife liv'd, upon
This day she was both pantler, butler, cook,
Both dame and servant; welcom'd all, serv'd all;
Would sing her song and dance her turn; now here
At upper end o'th' table, now i'th' middle;
On his shoulder, and his; her face o'fire
With labour, and the thing she took to quench it
She would to each one sip. You are retired,
As if you were a feasted one, and not
The hostess of the meeting: pray you, bid
These unknown friends to's welcome; for it is
A way to make us better friends, more known.
Come, quench your blushes, and present yourself
That which you are, Mistress o'th' Feast. Come on,
And bid us welcome to your sheep-shearing,
As your good flock shall prosper.

PERDITA [*to Polixenes*] Sir, welcome:
It is my father's will I should take on me
The hostess-ship o'th' day.
[*to Camillo*] You're welcome, sir.
Give me those flowers there, Dorcas. Reverend sirs,
For you, there's rosemary, and rue; these keep
Seeming and savour all the winter long:
Grace and remembrance be to you both,
And welcome to our shearing!

POLIXENES Shepherdess –
A fair one are you – well you fit our ages
With flowers of winter.

44

PERDITA Sir, the year growing ancient,
Not yet on summer's death nor on the birth
Of trembling winter, the fairest flowers o'th' season
Are our carnations and streak'd gillyvors,
Which some call nature's bastards: of that kind
Our rustic garden's barren; and I care not
To get slips of them.

POLIXENES Wherefore, gentle maiden,
Do you neglect them?

PERDITA For I have heard it said
There is an art which, in their piedness, shares
With great creating nature.

POLIXENES Say there be;
Yet nature is made better by no mean
But nature makes that mean: so, over that art,
Which you say adds to nature, is an art
That nature makes. You see, sweet maid, we marry
A gentler scion to the wildest stock,
And make conceive a bark of baser kind
By bud of nobler race. This is an art
Which does mend nature – change it rather – but
The art itself is nature.

PERDITA So it is.

POLIXENES Then make your garden rich in gillyvors,
And do not call them bastards.

PERDITA I'll not put
The dibble in earth to set one slip of them;
No more than, were I painted, I would wish
This youth should say 'twere well, and only therefore
Desire to breed by me. Here's flowers for you:
Hot lavender, mints, savory, marjoram,
The marigold, that goes to bed wi'th' sun
And with him rises, weeping: these are flowers
Of middle summer, and I think they are given
To men of middle age. Y'are very welcome.

[*She gives them flowers.*]

CAMILLO I should leave grazing, were I of your flock,
And only live by gazing.

PERDITA Out, alas!
You'd be so lean that blasts of January
Would blow you through and through.
[*to Florizel*] Now, my fair'st friend,
I would I had some flowers o'th' spring, that might
Become your time of day; and yours, and yours,
[*to Mopsa and the other girls*] That wear upon
    your virgin branches yet
Your maidenheads growing: O Proserpina,
For the flowers now that, frighted, thou let'st fall
From Dis's waggon! daffodils,
That come before the swallow dares, and take
The winds of March with beauty; violets, dim,
But sweeter than the lids of Juno's eyes
Or Cytherea's breath; pale primroses,
That die unmarried, ere they can behold
Bright Phoebus in his strength (a malady
Most incident to maids); bold oxlips and
The crown imperial; lilies of all kinds,
The flower-de-luce being one. O, these I lack,
To make you garlands of; and my sweet friend,
To strew him o'er and o'er!

FLORIZEL What, like a corpse?

PERDITA No, like a bank, for love to lie and play on:
Not like a corpse; or if – not to be buried,
But quick, and in mine arms. Come, take your flowers:
Methinks I play as I have seen them do
In Whitsun pastorals: sure this robe of mine
Does change my disposition.

FLORIZEL What you do,
Still betters what is done.

CYMBELINE

Written and first performed about 1610

Imogen, the daughter of Cymbeline, the King of Britain, has disguised herself as a young man and fled to escape from Cloten, the son of her stepmother by a previous marriage. She searches for her husband Posthumus, who has been tricked into believing that Imogen has committed adultery.

In disguise Imogen is befriended by Belarius, a lord banished many years earlier by Cymbeline, and by Cymbeline's sons Arviragus and Guiderius whom Belarius took with him as babies when he was banished. Cloten has pursued Imogen and has fought with Guiderius and been killed by him. Imogen has drunk a potion and is believed to be dead. Belarius, Arviragus and Guiderius resolve to inter Imogen and Cloten with the reverence due to a prince.

Act IV, ii (lines 258–81)

GUIDERIUS   Fear no more the heat o'th' sun,
         Nor the furious winter's rages,
   Thou thy worldly task has done,
        Home art gone and ta'en thy wages.
   Golden lads and girls all must,
   As chimney-sweepers, come to dust.

ARVIRAGUS   Fear no more the frown o'th' great,
         Thou art past the tyrant's stroke,
   Care no more to clothe and eat,
        To thee the reed is as the oak:
   The sceptre, learning, physic, must
   All follow this and come to dust.

GUIDERIUS   Fear no more the lightning-flash.
ARVIRAGUS   Nor th'all-dreaded thunder-stone.
GUIDERIUS   Fear not slander, censure rash.
ARVIRAGUS   Thou hast finish'd joy and moan.

BOTH   All lovers young, all lovers must
              Consign to thee and come to dust.

GUIDERIUS   No exorciser harm thee!
ARVIRAGUS   Nor no witchcraft charm thee!
GUIDERIUS   Ghost unlaid forbear thee!
ARVIRAGUS   Nothing ill come near thee!
BOTH   Quiet consummation have,
              And renowned be thy grave!

THE TEMPEST

....

Written and first performed 1610–11

Twelve years earlier Prospero, Duke of Milan, was ousted by his brother Antonio. With the help of Alonso, King of Naples, Antonio had Prospero and his infant daughter Miranda abandoned at sea in a rotten boat. They came to shore on an island inhabited by the creature Caliban.

Prospero curses Caliban while Caliban complains of his enslavement to him.

Act I, ii (lines 321–53)

PROSPERO Thou poisonous slave, got by the devil himself
Upon thy wicked dam, come forth!

Enter CALIBAN.

CALIBAN As wicked dew as e'er my mother brush'd
With raven's feather from unwholesome fen
Drop on you both! a south-west blow on ye
And blister you all o'er!

PROSPERO For this, be sure, to-night thou shalt have cramps,
Side-stitches that shall pen thy breath up; urchins
Shall, for that vast of night that they may work,
All exercise on thee; thou shalt be pinch'd
As thick as honeycomb, each pinch more stinging
Than bees that made 'em.

CALIBAN I must eat my dinner.
This island's mine, by Sycorax my mother,
Which thou tak'st from me. When thou cam'st first,
Thou strok'st me, and made much of me; wouldst give me
Water with berries in 't; and teach me how
To name the bigger light, and how the less,
That burn by day and night: and then I lov'd thee,
And show'd thee all the qualities o'th' isle,

The fresh springs, brine-pits, barren place and fertile:
Curs'd be I that did so! All the charms
Of Sycorax, toads, beetles, bats, light on you!
For I am all the subjects that you have,
Which first was mine own King: and here you sty me
In this hard rock, whiles you do keep from me
The rest o'th' island.

PROSPERO Thou most lying slave,
Whom stripes may move, not kindness! I have us'd thee,
Filth as thou art, with human care; and lodg'd thee
In mine own cell, till thou didst seek to violate
The honour of my child.

CALIBAN O ho, O ho! would't had been done!
Thou didst prevent me; I had peopled else
This isle with Calibans.

By fortune and Prospero's magic arts, Alonso, Antonio, his son Ferdinand, and others from Naples and Milan have been cast ashore on the island. Ariel, Prospero's chief spirit, draws Ferdinand on.

Act I, ii (lines 377–407)

Ariel's Song.

ARIEL Come unto these yellow sands,
     And then take hands:
    Courtsied when you have and kiss'd
     The wild waves whist:
    Foot it featly here and there,
     And sweet sprites bear
    The burthen. Hark, hark.
[*burthen dispersedly*] Bow-wow.

ARIEL The watch dogs bark:
[*burthen dispersedly*] Bow-wow.

ARIEL Hark, hark! I hear
    The strain of strutting chanticleer
    Cry
[*burthen dispersedly*] Cock a diddle dow.

FERDINAND Where should this music be? i'th' air or th' earth?
It sounds no more: and, sure, it waits upon
Some god o'th' island. Sitting on a bank,
Weeping again the King my father's wrack,
This music crept by me upon the waters,
Allaying both their fury and my passion
With its sweet air: thence I have follow'd it,
Or it hath drawn me rather. But 'tis gone.
No, it begins again.
       Ariel's Song.

ARIEL Full fadom five thy father lies;
    Of his bones are coral made;
    Those are pearls that were his eyes:
     Nothing of him that doth fade,
    But doth suffer a sea-change
    Into something rich and strange.
    Sea-nymphs hourly ring his knell:
[*burthen*] Ding-dong.
ARIEL Hark! now I hear them, – Ding-dong, bell.

Trinculo, a seaman, stumbles across Caliban.

Act II,'ii (lines 18–40)

TRINCULO Here's neither bush nor shrub, to bear off any weather at all, and another storm brewing; I hear it sing i'th' wind: yond same black cloud, yond huge one, looks like a foul bombard that would shed his liquor. If it should thunder as it did before, I know not where to hide my head: yond same cloud cannot choose but fall by pailfuls. What have we here? a man or a fish? dead or alive? A fish: he smells like a fish; a very ancient and fish-like smell; a kind of, not of the newest Poor-John. A strange fish! Were I in England now, as once I was, and had but this fish painted, not a holiday fool there but would give a piece of silver: there would this monster make a man; any strange beast there makes a man: when they will not give a doit to relieve a lame beggar, they will lay out ten to see a dead Indian. Legg'd like a man! and his fins like arms! Warm o' my troth! I do now let loose my opinion, hold it no longer: this is no fish, but an islander, that hath lately suffered by a thunderbolt. [*thunder*] Alas, the storm is come again! my best way is to creep under his gaberdine; there is no other shelter hereabout: misery acquaints a man with strange bed-fellows. I will here shroud till the dregs of the storm be past.

Caliban has hatched a plot with Stephano and Trinculo to kill Prospero and take Miranda. Ariel, who is watching them for Prospero, has played a tune and frightened the seamen. Caliban reassures them.

Act III, ii (lines 135–45)

CALIBAN Art thou afeard?

STEPHANO No, monster, not I.

CALIBAN Be not afeard; the isle is full of noises,
Sounds and sweet airs, that give delight, and hurt not.
Sometimes a thousand twangling instruments
Will hum about mine ears; and sometime voices,
That, if I then had wak'd after long sleep,
Will make me sleep again: and then, in dreaming,
The clouds methought would open, and show riches
Ready to drop upon me; that, when I wak'd,
I cried to dream again.

As planned by Prospero, Ferdinand and Miranda have fallen in love. Prospero celebrates their engagement with them, but then, recalling Caliban's plot, breaks off the celebrations.

Act IV, i (lines 146–63)

PROSPERO You do look, my son, in a mov'd sort,
As if you were dismay'd: be cheerful, sir.
Our revels now are ended. These our actors,
As I foretold you, were all spirits, and
Are melted into air, into thin air:
And, like the baseless fabric of this vision,
The cloud-capp'd towers, the gorgeous palaces,
The solemn temples, the great globe itself,
Yea, all which it inherit, shall dissolve,
And, like this insubstantial pageant faded,
Leave not a rack behind. We are such stuff
As dreams are made on; and our little life
Is rounded with a sleep. Sir, I am vex'd;
Bear with my weakness; my old brain is troubled:
Be not disturb'd with my infirmity:
If you be pleas'd, retire into my cell,
And there repose: a turn or two I'll walk,
To still my beating mind.

Tragedies

— ◇ —

ROMEO AND JULIET

Written and first performed 1594

*In Verona, Romeo is the only son of the nobleman Montague;
Juliet is the daughter of the nobleman Capulet. The two families are
at feud with each other. The play's Prologue invites the audience
to see and hear the young couple's tragic story.*

Prologue

Enter CHORUS.

CHORUS Two households both alike in dignity
(In fair Verona, where we lay our scene)
From ancient grudge break to new mutiny,
Where civil blood makes civil hands unclean.
From forth the fatal loins of these two foes
A pair of star-cross'd lovers take their life,
Whose misadventur'd piteous overthrows
Doth with their death bury their parents' strife.
The fearful passage of their death-mark'd love
And the continuance of their parents' rage,
Which, but their children's end, nought could remove,
Is now the two hours' traffic of our stage;
The which, if you with patient ears attend,
What here shall miss, our toil shall strive to mend.

Romeo, together with his friend Mercutio and cousin Benvolio, has invited himself to a feast at the Capulets' house. There he sees Juliet and instantly falls in love with her.

Act I, v (lines 44–53)

ROMEO O, she doth teach the torches to burn bright.
It seems she hangs upon the cheek of night
As a rich jewel in an Ethiop's ear –
Beauty too rich for use, for earth too dear.
So shows a snowy dove trooping with crows
As yonder lady o'er her fellows shows.
The measure done, I'll watch her place of stand,
And touching hers, make blessed my rude hand.
Did my heart love till now? Forswear it, sight.
For I ne'er saw true beauty till this night.

Romeo and Juliet have briefly met and kissed at the feast;
Juliet returns Romeo's love. After the feast, Romeo waits outside
Juliet's chamber in the hope of seeing her. Juliet appears.

Act II, ii (lines 2–49)

ROMEO But soft, what light through yonder window breaks?
It is the east and Juliet is the sun!
Arise fair sun and kill the envious moon
Who is already sick and pale with grief
That thou her maid art far more fair than she.
Be not her maid since she is envious,
Her vestal livery is but sick and green
And none but fools do wear it. Cast it off.
It is my lady, O it is my love!
O that she knew she were!
She speaks, yet she says nothing. What of that?
Her eye discourses, I will answer it.
I am too bold. 'Tis not to me she speaks.
Two of the fairest stars in all the heaven,
Having some business, do entreat her eyes
To twinkle in their spheres till they return.
What if her eyes were there, they in her head?
The brightness of her cheek would shame those stars
As daylight doth a lamp. Her eyes in heaven
Would through the airy region stream so bright
That birds would sing and think it were not night.
See how she leans her cheek upon her hand.
O that I were a glove upon that hand,
That I might touch that cheek.

JULIET Ay me.

ROMEO She speaks.
O speak again bright angel, for thou art
As glorious to this night, being o'er my head,
As is a winged messenger of heaven
Unto the white-upturned wondering eyes
Of mortals that fall back to gaze on him

When he bestrides the lazy-puffing clouds
And sails upon the bosom of the air.

JULIET O Romeo, Romeo, wherefore art thou Romeo?
Deny thy father and refuse thy name.
Or if thou wilt not, be but sworn my love
And I'll no longer be a Capulet.

ROMEO Shall I hear more, or shall I speak at this?

JULIET 'Tis but thy name that is my enemy:
Thou art thyself, though not a Montague.
What's Montague? It is nor hand nor foot
Nor arm nor face nor any other part
Belonging to a man. O be some other name.
What's in a name? That which we call a rose
By any other word would smell as sweet;
So Romeo would, were he not Romeo call'd,
Retain that dear perfection which he owes
Without that title. Romeo, doff thy name,
And for thy name, which is no part of thee,
Take all myself.

Romeo and Juliet promise lasting love to each other. As day approaches Romeo leaves to arrange their secret wedding.

Act II, ii (lines 176–91)

JULIET 'Tis almost morning, I would have thee gone,
And yet no farther than a wanton's bird,
That lets it hop a little from his hand
Like a poor prisoner in his twisted gyves,
And with a silken thread plucks it back again,
So loving-jealous of his liberty.

ROMEO I would I were thy bird.

JULIET Sweet, so would I:
Yet I should kill thee with much cherishing.
Good night, good night. Parting is such sweet sorrow
That I shall say good night till it be morrow.

Exit Juliet.

ROMEO Sleep dwell upon thine eyes, peace in thy breast.
Would I were sleep and peace so sweet to rest.
The grey-ey'd morn smiles on the frowning night,
Chequering the eastern clouds with streaks of light;
And darkness fleckled like a drunkard reels
From forth day's pathway, made by Titan's wheels.

Tybalt, Juliet's cousin, and his companion Petruchio come upon Mercutio and Benvolio. As they prepare to fight, Romeo arrives and tries to separate them. Tybalt fatally wounds Mercutio.

Act III, i (lines 91–109)

MERCUTIO I am hurt.
A plague o' both your houses. I am sped.
Is he gone, and hath nothing?

BENVOLIO What, art thou hurt?

MERCUTIO Ay, ay, a scratch, a scratch. Marry, 'tis enough.
Where is my page? Go villian, fetch a surgeon.

> *Exit Page.*

ROMEO Courage, man, the hurt cannot be much.

MERCUTIO No, 'tis not so deep as a well, nor so wide as a church door, but 'tis enough, 'twill serve. Ask for me tomorrow and you shall find me a grave man. I am peppered, I warrant, for this world. A plague o' both your houses. Zounds, a dog, a rat, a mouse, a cat, to scratch a man to death. A braggart, a rogue, a villain, that fights by the book of arithmetic – why the devil came you between us? I was hurt under your arm.

ROMEO I thought all for the best.

MERCUTIO Help me into some house, Benvolio,
Or I shall faint. A plague o' both your houses,
They have made worms' meat of me.
I have it, and soundly too. Your houses!

Juliet and Romeo have secretly married. That night, unaware that Romeo has killed her cousin Tybalt, Juliet waits for Romeo to return.

Act III, ii (lines 1–25)

JULIET Gallop apace, you fiery-footed steeds,
Towards Phoebus' lodging. Such a waggoner
As Phaeton would whip you to the west
And bring in cloudy night immediately.
Spread thy close curtain, love-performing night,
That runaway's eyes may wink, and Romeo
Leap to these arms untalk'd-of and unseen.
Lovers can see to do their amorous rites
By their own beauties; or, if love be blind,
It best agrees with night. Come, civil night,
Thou sober-suited matron, all in black,
And learn me how to lose a winning match
Play'd for a pair of stainless maidenhoods.
Hood my unmann'd blood, bating in my cheeks,
With thy black mantle, till strange love grow bold,
Think true love acted simple modesty.
Come night, come Romeo, come thou day in night,
For thou wilt lie upon the wings of night
Whiter than new snow upon a raven's back.
Come gentler night, come loving black-brow'd night,
Give me my Romeo; and when I shall die
Take him and cut him out in little stars,
And he will make the face of heaven so fine
That all the world will be in love with night,
And pay no worship to the garish sun.

The Prince of Verona has banished Romeo for killing Tybalt. Romeo and Juliet secretly share their wedding night before Romeo flees Verona.

Act III, v (lines 1–36)

JULIET Wilt thou be gone? It is not yet near day.
It was the nightingale and not the lark
That pierc'd the fearful hollow of thine ear.
Nightly she sings on yond pomegranate tree.
Believe me, love, it was the nightingale.

ROMEO It was the lark, the herald of the morn,
No nightingale. Look, love, what envious streaks
Do lace the severing clouds in yonder east.
Night's candles are burnt out, and jocund day
Stands tiptoe on the misty mountain tops.
I must be gone and live, or stay and die.

JULIET Yond light is not daylight, I know it, I.
It is some meteor that the sun exhales
To be to thee this night a torchbearer
And light thee on thy way to Mantua.
Therefore stay yet: thou need'st not to be gone.

ROMEO Let me be ta'en, let me be put to death,
I am content, so thou wilt have it so.
I'll say yon grey is not the morning's eye,
'Tis but the pale reflex of Cynthia's brow.
Nor that is not the lark whose notes do beat
The vaulty heaven so high above our heads.
I have more care to stay than will to go.
Come death, and welcome. Juliet wills it so.
How is't, my soul? Let's talk. It is not day.

JULIET It is, it is. Hie hence, begone, away.
It is the lark that sings so out of tune,
Straining harsh discords and unpleasing sharps.
Some say the lark makes sweet division.
This doth not so, for she divideth us.

Some say the lark and loathed toad change eyes.
O, now I would they had chang'd voices too,
Since arm from arm that voice doth us affray,
Hunting thee hence with hunt's-up to the day.
O now be gone, more light and light it grows.

ROMEO More light and light: more dark and dark our woes.

Juliet has drunk a potion, which has sent her to sleep for twenty-four hours. She appears to be dead. Romeo does not know about the potion and when he finds Juliet asleep, he believes that she is dead.

Act V, iii (lines 87–115)

ROMEO Death, lie thou there, by a dead man interr'd.
How oft when men are at the point of death
Have they been merry! Which their keepers call
A lightning before death. O how may I
Call this a lightning? O my love, my wife,
Death that hath suck'd the honey of thy breath
Hath had no power yet upon thy beauty.
Thou art not conquer'd. Beauty's ensign yet
Is crimson in thy lips and in thy cheeks,
And Death's pale flag is not advanced there.
Tybalt, liest thou there in thy bloody sheet?
O, what more favour can I do to thee
Than with that hand that cut thy youth in twain
To sunder his that was thine enemy?
Forgive me, cousin. Ah, dear Juliet,
Why art thou yet so fair? Shall I believe
That unsubstantial Death is amorous,
And that the lean abhorred monster keeps
Thee here in dark to be his paramour?
For fear of that I still will stay with thee,
And never from this palace of dim night
Depart again. Here, here, will I remain
With worms that are thy chambermaids. O here
Will I set up my everlasting rest
And shake the yoke of inauspicious stars
From this world-wearied flesh. Eyes, look your last.
Arms, take your last embrace! And lips, O you
The doors of breath, seal with a righteous kiss
A dateless bargain to engrossing Death.

JULIUS CAESAR

Written and first performed 1599

*In republican Rome Julius Caesar's power is growing, and some
senators fear that he will be made king. On his way to the Capitol
Caesar is called to by a soothsayer.*

Act I, ii (lines 12–24)

SOOTHSAYER Caesar!

CAESAR Ha! Who calls?

CASCA Bid every noise be still; peace yet again!

CAESAR Who is it in the press that calls on me?
I hear a tongue shriller than all the music
Cry 'Caesar!' Speak. Caesar is turn'd to hear.

SOOTHSAYER Beware the ides of March.

CAESAR What man is that?

BRUTUS A soothsayer bids you beware the ides of March.

CAESAR Set him before me; let me see his face.

CASSIUS Fellow, come from the throng; look upon Caesar.

CAESAR What say'st thou to me now? Speak once again.

SOOTHSAYER Beware the ides of March.

CAESAR He is a dreamer. Let us leave him. Pass.

While Caesar is at the Capitol, Cassius discusses Caesar's ascendancy with Brutus, his fellow senator.

Act I, ii (lines 130–59)

BRUTUS Another general shout?
I do believe that these applauses are
For some new honours that are heap'd on Caesar.

CASSIUS Why, man, he doth bestride the narrow world
Like a Colossus, and we petty men
Walk under his huge legs, and peep about
To find ourselves dishonourable graves.
Men at some time are masters of their fates:
The fault, dear Brutus, is not in our stars,
But in ourselves, that we are underlings.
Brutus and Caesar: what should be in that 'Caesar'?
Why should that name be sounded more than yours?
Write them together, yours is as fair a name;
Sound them, it doth become the mouth as well;
Weigh them, it is as heavy; conjure with 'em,
'Brutus' will start a spirit as soon as 'Caesar'.
Now in the names of all the gods at once,
Upon what meat doth this our Caesar feed,
That he is grown so great? Age, thou art sham'd!
Rome, thou hast lost the breed of noble bloods!
When went there by an age, since the great flood,
But it was fam'd with more than with one man?
When could they say, till now, that talk'd of Rome,
That her wide walks encompass'd but one man?
Now is it Rome indeed, and room enough,
When there is in it but one only man.
O, you and I have heard our fathers say,
There was a Brutus once that would have brook'd
Th' eternal devil to keep his state in Rome
As easily as a king.

At night Cassius goes with some other senators to Brutus's house,
where they agree that Caesar shall be killed. When they leave,
Portia, Brutus's wife, goes to Brutus.

Act II, i (lines 260–87)

BRUTUS Good Portia, go to bed.

PORTIA Is Brutus sick, and is it physical
To walk unbraced and suck up the humours
Of the dank morning? What, is Brutus sick?
And will he steal out of his wholesome bed
To dare the vile contagion of the night,
And tempt the rheumy and unpurged air
To add unto his sickness? No, my Brutus;
You have some sick offence within your mind,
Which, by the right and virtue of my place,
I ought to know of; and, upon my knees,
I charm you, by my once commended beauty,
By all your vows of love, and that great vow
Which did incorporate and make us one,
That you unfold to me, your self, your half,
Why you are heavy, and what men to-night
Have had resort to you; for here have been
Some six or seven, who did hide their faces
Even from darkness.

BRUTUS Kneel not, gentle Portia.

PORTIA I should not need, if you were gentle Brutus.
Within the bond of marriage, tell me, Brutus,
Is it excepted I should know no secrets
That appertain to you? Am I your self
But, as it were, in sort or limitation,
To keep with you at meals, comfort your bed,
And talk to you sometimes? Dwell I but in the suburbs
Of your good pleasure? If it be no more,
Portia is Brutus' harlot, not his wife.

On the ides of March Calphurnia, Caesar's wife, urges Caesar to stay at home because the omens are bad.

Act II, ii (lines 8–37)

CALPHURNIA What mean you, Caesar? Think you to walk forth
You shall not stir out of your house to-day.

CAESAR Caesar shall forth. The things that threaten'd me
Ne'er look'd but on my back; when they shall see
The face of Caesar, they are vanished.

CALPHURNIA Caesar, I never stood on ceremonies,
Yet now they fright me. There is one within,
Besides the things that we have heard and seen,
Recounts most horrid sights seen by the watch.
A lioness hath whelped in the streets,
And graves have yawn'd and yielded up their dead;
Fierce fiery warriors fight upon the clouds
In ranks and squadrons and right form of war,
Which drizzled blood upon the Capitol;
The noise of battle hurtled in the air,
Horses did neigh, and dying men did groan,
And ghosts did shriek and squeal about the streets.
O Caesar, these things are beyond all use,
And I do fear them.

CAESAR What can be avoided
Whose end is purpos'd by the mighty gods?
Yet Caesar shall go forth; for these predictions
Are to the world in general as to Caesar.

CALPHURNIA When beggars die, there are no comets seen;
The heavens themselves blaze forth the death of princes.

CAESAR Cowards die many times before their deaths;
The valiant never taste of death but once.
Of all the wonders that I yet have heard,
It seems to me most strange that men should fear,
Seeing that death, a necessary end,
Will come when it will come.

Caesar is at the Senate. He rejects an appeal for clemency and the conspirators seize the opportunity to stab him.

Act III, i (lines 58–78)

CAESAR I could be well mov'd, if I were as you;
If I could pray to move, prayers would move me;
But I am constant as the northern star,
Of whose true-fix'd and resting quality
There is no fellow in the firmament.
The skies are painted with unnumber'd sparks,
They are all fire, and every one doth shine;
But there's but one in all doth hold his place.
So in the world: 'tis furnish'd well with men,
And men are flesh and blood, and apprehensive;
Yet in the number I do know but one
That unassailable holds on his rank,
Unshak'd of motion; and that I am he,
Let me a little show it, even in this,
That I was constant Cimber should be banish'd,
And constant do remain to keep him so.

CINNA O Caesar –

CAESAR Hence! Wilt thou lift up Olympus?

DECIUS Great Caesar –

CAESAR Doth not Brutus bootless kneel?

CASCA Speak hands for me! [*They stab Caesar.*]

CAESAR *Et tu, Brute?* – Then fall Caesar! [*Dies.*]

Brutus has explained to the Roman citizens why the conspirators killed Caesar, and they have accepted his argument. Mark Antony now ascends the pulpit to make his tribute to Caesar.

Act III, ii (lines 74–108)

ANTONY Friends, Romans, countrymen, lend me your ears;
I come to bury Caesar, not to praise him.
The evil that men do lives after them,
The good is oft interred with their bones;
So let it be with Caesar. The noble Brutus
Hath told you Caesar was ambitious.
If it were so, it was a grievous fault,
And grievously hath Caesar answer'd it.
Here, under leave of Brutus and the rest,
(For Brutus is an honourable man,
So are they all, all honourable men)
Come I to speak in Caesar's funeral.
He was my friend, faithful and just to me;
But Brutus says he was ambitious,
And Brutus is an honourable man.
He hath brought many captives home to Rome,
Whose ransoms did the general coffers fill:
Did this in Caesar seem ambitious?
When that the poor have cried, Caesar hath wept;
Ambition should be made of sterner stuff:
Yet Brutus says he was ambitious,
And Brutus is an honourable man.
You all did see that on the Lupercal
I thrice presented him a kingly crown,
Which he did thrice refuse. Was this ambition?
Yet Brutus says he was ambitious,
And sure he is an honourable man.
I speak not to disprove what Brutus spoke,
But here I am to speak what I do know.
You all did love him once, not without cause;
What cause withholds you then to mourn for him?

O judgment, thou art fled to brutish beasts,
And men have lost their reason. Bear with me.
My heart is in the coffin there with Caesar,
And I must pause till it come back to me.

As the Roman citizens transfer their sympathies to Caesar,
Mark Antony invites them to look at the body.

Act III, ii (lines 170–98)

ANTONY If you have tears, prepare to shed them now.
You all do know this mantle. I remember
The first time ever Caesar put it on;
'Twas on a summer's evening in his tent,
That day he overcame the Nervii.
Look, in this place ran Cassius' dagger through:
See what a rent the envious Casca made:
Through this the well-beloved Brutus stabb'd;
And as he pluck'd his cursed steel away,
Mark how the blood of Caesar follow'd it,
As rushing out of doors, to be resolv'd
If Brutus so unkindly knock'd or no;
For Brutus, as you know, was Caesar's angel.
Judge, O you gods, how dearly Caesar lov'd him.
This was the most unkindest cut of all;
For when the noble Caesar saw him stab,
Ingratitude, more strong than traitors' arms,
Quite vanquish'd him: then burst his mighty heart;
And in his mantle muffling up his face,
Even at the base of Pompey's statue
(Which all the while ran blood) great Caesar fell.
O, what a fall was there, my countrymen!
Then I, and you, and all of us fell down,
Whilst bloody treason flourish'd over us.
O, now you weep, and I perceive you feel
The dint of pity. These are gracious drops.
Kind souls, what weep you when you but behold
Our Caesar's vesture wounded? Look you here!
Here is himself, marr'd, as you see, with traitors.

The conspirators flee Rome. Together with Octavius Caesar,
Julius Caesar's son, Mark Antony has raised an army and pursued
them to Philippi, where he defeats them in battle. Cassius and
Brutus kill themselves. Mark Antony pays tribute to Brutus.

Act V, v (lines 68–75)

ANTONY This was the noblest Roman of them all.
All the conspirators save only he
Did that they did in envy of great Caesar;
He only, in a general honest thought
And common good to all, made one of them.
His life was gentle, and the elements
So mix'd in him, that Nature might stand up
And say to all the world, 'This was a man!'

HAMLET

....

Written and first performed 1600

In Denmark the death of the King has been swiftly followed by the marriage of his widow Gertrude to his brother Claudius, the new King. A ghost resembling the dead King has been seen by the royal guards on the castle walls at Elsinore. They ask Horatio, a confidant of Prince Hamlet, the son of Gertrude and the dead King, to witness it. The ghost appears, then disappears as the cock crows.

Act I, i (lines 152–78)

BARNARDO It was about to speak when the cock crew.

HORATIO And then it started like a guilty thing
Upon a fearful summons. I have heard
The cock, that is the trumpet to the morn,
Doth with his lofty and shrill-sounding throat
Awake the god of day, and at his warning,
Whether in sea or fire, in earth or air,
Th'extravagant and erring spirit hies
To his confine; and of the truth herein
This present object made probation.

MARCELLUS It faded on the crowing of the cock.
Some say that ever 'gainst that season comes
Wherein our Saviour's birth is celebrated,
This bird of dawning singeth all night long;
And then, they say, no spirit dare stir abroad,
The nights are wholesome, then no planets strike,
No fairy takes, nor witch hath power to charm,
So hallow'd and so gracious is that time.

HORATIO So have I heard and do in part believe it.
But look, the morn in russet mantle clad
Walks o'er the dew of yon high eastward hill.
Break we our watch up, and by my advice
Let us impart what we have seen tonight

Unto young Hamlet; for upon my life
This spirit, dumb to us, will speak to him.
Do you consent we shall acquaint him with it
As needful in our loves, fitting our duty?

At the royal court the rites of mourning have been set aside for the wedding celebrations of King Claudius and Gertrude. Claudius has asked Hamlet to remain at court, rather than return to his studies at Wittenberg, and Hamlet agrees to do so. Alone, he rages against the recent events.

Act I, ii (lines 129–59)

HAMLET O that this too too sullied flesh would melt,
Thaw and resolve itself into a dew,
Or that the Everlasting had not fix'd
His canon 'gainst self-slaughter. O God! God!
How weary, stale, flat, and unprofitable
Seem to me all the uses of this world!
Fie on't, ah fie, 'tis an unweeded garden
That grows to seed; things rank and gross in nature
Possess it merely. That it should come to this!
But two months dead – nay, not so much, not two –
So excellent a king, that was to this
Hyperion to a satyr, so loving to my mother
That he might not beteem the winds of heaven
Visit her face too roughly. Heaven and earth,
Must I remember? Why, she would hang on him
As if increase of appetite had grown
By what it fed on; and yet within a month –
Let me not think on't – Frailty, thy name is woman –
A little month, or ere those shoes were old
With which she follow'd my poor father's body,
Like Niobe, all tears – why, she –
O God, a beast that wants discourse of reason
Would have mourn'd longer – married with my uncle,
My father's brother – but no more like my father
Than I to Hercules. Within a month,
Ere yet the salt of most unrighteous tears
Had left the flushing in her galled eyes,
She married – O most wicked speed! To post
With such dexterity to incestuous sheets!
It is not, nor it cannot come to good.
But break, my heart, for I must hold my tongue.

*The courtier Polonius has two children, Laertes, who lives in France,
and Ophelia. Having returned to Denmark for the wedding
celebrations, Laertes is about to go back to France. His father
counsels him.*

Act I, iii (lines 55–81)

POLONIUS Yet here, Laertes? Aboard, aboard for shame.
The wind sits in the shoulder of your sail,
And you are stay'd for. There, my blessing with thee.
And these few precepts in thy memory
Look thou character. Give thy thoughts no tongue,
Nor any unproportion'd thought his act.
Be thou familiar, but by no means vulgar;
Those friends thou hast, and their adoption tried,
Grapple them unto thy soul with hoops of steel,
But do not dull thy palm with entertainment
Of each new-hatch'd, unfledg'd courage. Beware
Of entrance to a quarrel, but being in,
Bear't that th'opposed may beware of thee.
Give every man thy ear, but few thy voice;
Take each man's censure, but reserve thy judgment.
Costly thy habit as thy purse can buy,
But not express'd in fancy; rich, not gaudy;
For the apparel oft proclaims the man,
And they in France of the best rank and station
Are of a most select and generous chief in that.
Neither a borrower nor a lender be,
For loan oft loses both itself and friend,
And borrowing dulls the edge of husbandry.
This above all: to thine own self be true,
And it must follow as the night the day
Thou canst not then be false to any man.
Farewell, my blessing season this in thee.

King Claudius has sent for two former schoolfriends of Hamlet, Rosencrantz and Guildenstern, in order to discover why Hamlet's demeanour has changed. Hamlet realises that his friends are acting on the King's behalf.

Act II, ii (lines 294–310)

GUILDENSTERN My Lord, we were sent for.

HAMLET I will tell you why; so shall my anticipation prevent your discovery, and your secrecy to the King and Queen moult no feather. I have of late, but wherefore I know not, lost all my mirth, forgone all custom of exercises; and indeed it goes so heavily with my disposition that this goodly frame the earth seems to me a sterile promontory, this most excellent canopy the air, look you, this brave o'erhanging firmament, this majestical roof fretted with golden fire, why, it appeareth nothing to me but a foul and pestilent congregation of vapours. What piece of work is a man, how noble in reason, how infinite in faculties, in form and moving how express and admirable, in action how like an angel, in apprehension how like a god: the beauty of the world, the paragon of animals – and yet, to me, what is this quintessence of dust? Man delights not me – nor woman neither, though by your smiling you seem to say so.

Hamlet considers whether he should take action, or not, to right the murder of his father.

Act III, i (lines 56–89)

HAMLET To be, or not to be, that is the question:
Whether 'tis nobler in the mind to suffer
The slings and arrows of outrageous fortune,
Or to take arms against a sea of troubles
And by opposing end them. To die – to sleep,
No more; and by a sleep to say we end
The heart-ache and the thousand natural shocks
That flesh is heir to: 'tis a consummation
Devoutly to be wish'd. To die, to sleep;
To sleep, perchance to dream – ay, there's the rub:
For in that sleep of death what dreams may come,
When we have shuffled off this mortal coil,
Must give us pause – there's the respect
That makes calamity of so long life.
For who would bear the whips and scorns of time,
Th'oppressor's wrong, the proud man's contumely,
The pangs of dispriz'd love, the law's delay,
The insolence of office, and the spurns
That patient merit of th'unworthy takes,
When he himself might his quietus make
With a bare bodkin? Who would fardels bear,
To grunt and sweat under a weary life,
But that the dread of something after death,
The undiscover'd country, from whose bourn
No traveller returns, puzzles the will,
And makes us rather bear those ills we have
Than fly to others that we know not of?
Thus conscience does make cowards of us all,
And thus the native hue of resolution
Is sicklied o'er with the pale cast of thought,
And enterprises of great pitch and moment
With this regard their currents turn awry
And lose the name of action. Soft you now,
The fair Ophelia! Nymph, in thy orisons
Be all my sins remember'd.

Polonius believes that Hamlet is acting strangely because he is in love with Ophelia. On Polonius's advice the King sends Ophelia to speak to Hamlet, but he does not respond as expected.

Act III, i (lines 121–162)

HAMLET Get thee to a nunnery. Why, wouldst thou be a breeder of sinners? I am myself indifferent honest, but yet I could accuse me of such things that it were better my mother had not borne me. I am very proud, revengeful, ambitious, with more offences at my beck than I have thoughts to put them in, imagination to give them shape, or time to act them in. What should such fellows as I do crawling between earth and heaven? We are arrant knaves all, believe none of us. Go thy ways to a nunnery. Where's your father?

OPHELIA At home, my lord.

HAMLET Let the doors be shut upon him, that he may play the fool nowhere but in's own house. Farewell.

OPHELIA O help him, you sweet heavens.

HAMLET If thou dost marry, I'll give thee this plague for thy dowry: be thou as chaste as ice, as pure as snow, thou shalt not escape calumny. Get thee to a nunnery, farewell. Or if thou wilt needs marry, marry a fool; for wise men know well enough what monsters you make of them. To a nunnery, go – and quickly too. Farewell.

OPHELIA Heavenly powers, restore him.

HAMLET I have heard of your paintings well enough. God hath given you one face and you make yourselves another. You jig and amble, and you lisp, you nickname God's creatures, and make your wantonness your ignorance. Go to, I'll no more on't, it hath made me mad. I say we will have no mo marriage. Those that are married already – all but one – shall live; the rest shall keep as they are. To a nunnery, go. *Exit.*

OPHELIA O, what a noble mind is here o'erthrown!
The courtier's, soldier's, scholar's, eye, tongue, sword,
Th'expectancy and rose of the fair state,
The glass of fashion and the mould of form,
Th'observ'd of all observers, quite, quite down!
And I, of ladies most deject and wretched,
That suck'd the honey of his music vows,
Now see that noble and most sovereign reason
Like sweet bells jangled out of tune and harsh,
That unmatch'd form and feature of blown youth
Blasted with ecstasy. O woe is me
T'have seen what I have seen, see what I see.

A group of players has arrived at the court. To test out what the ghost has told him, Hamlet instructs the players to enact the murder of his father.

Act III, ii (lines 1–46)

HAMLET Speak the speech, I pray you, as I pronounced it to you, trippingly on the tongue; but if you mouth it as many of your players do, I had as lief the town-crier spoke my lines. Nor do not saw the air too much with your hand, thus, but use all gently; for in the very torrent, tempest, and, as I may say, whirl-wind of your passion, you must acquire and beget a temperance that may give it smoothness. O, it offends me to the soul to hear a robustious periwig-pated fellow tear a passion to tatters, to very rags, to split the ears of the groundlings, who for the most part are capable of nothing but inexplicable dumb-shows and noise. I would have such a fellow whipped for o'erdoing Termagant. It out-Herods Herod. Pray you avoid it.

1 PLAYER I warrant your honour.

HAMLET Be not too tame neither, but let your own discretion be your tutor. Suit the action to the word, the word to the action, with this special observance, that you o'erstep not the modesty of nature. For anything so o'erdone is from the purpose of playing, whose end, both at the first and now, was and is to hold as 'twere the mirror up to nature; to show virtue her feature, scorn her own image, and the very age and body of the time his form and pressure. Now this overdone or come tardy off, though it makes the unskilful laugh, cannot but make the judicious grieve, the censure of the which one must in your allowance o'erweigh a whole theatre of others. O, there be players that I have seen play – and heard others praise, and that highly – not to speak it profanely, that neither having th'accent of Christians, nor the gait of Christian, pagan, nor man, have so strutted and bellowed that I have thought some of Nature's journeymen had made men, and not made them well, they imitated humanity so abominably.

1 PLAYER I hope we have reformed that indifferently with us.

HAMLET O reform it altogether. And let those that play your clowns speak no more than is set down for them – for there be of them that will themselves laugh, to set on some quantity of barren spectators to laugh too, though in the meantime some necessary question of the play be then to be considered. That's villainous, and show a most pitiful ambition in the fool that uses it. Go make you ready.

Exeunt Players.

Gertrude has called Hamlet to her chamber, where she has installed Polonius behind a tapestry to eavesdrop on the conversation. Hearing a noise from behind the tapestry, Hamlet has killed Polonius. Gertrude challenges Hamlet over Polonius's death, but Hamlet rebukes her with her treachery to his father, her late husband.

Act III, iv (lines 53–88)

HAMLET Look here upon this picture, and on this,
The counterfeit presentment of two brothers.
See what a grace was seated on this brow,
Hyperion's curls, the front of Jove himself,
An eye like Mars to threaten and command,
A station like the herald Mercury
New-lighted on a heaven-kissing hill,
A combination and a form indeed
Where every god did seem to set his seal
To give the world assurance of a man.
This was your husband. Look you now what follows.
Here is your husband, like a mildew'd ear
Blasting his wholesome brother. Have you eyes?
Could you on this fair mountain leave to feed
And batten on this moor? Ha, have you eyes?
You cannot call it love; for at your age
The heyday in the blood is tame, it's humble,
And waits upon the judgment, and what judgment
Would step from this to this? Sense sure you have,
Else could you not have motion; but sure that sense
Is apoplex'd, for madness would not err
Nor sense to ecstasy was ne'er so thrall'd
But it reserv'd some quantity of choice
To serve in such a difference. What devil was't
That thus hath cozen'd you at hoodman blind?
Eyes without feeling, feeling without sight,
Ears without hands or eyes, smelling sans all,
Or but a sickly part of one true sense
Could not so mope. O shame, where is thy blush?

Rebellious hell,
If thou canst mutine in a matron's bones,
To flaming youth let virtue be as wax
And melt in her own fire; proclaim no shame
When the compulsive ardour gives the charge,
Since frost itself as actively doth burn
And reason panders will.

Laertes has secretly returned from France to avenge his father's death. As the King continues to turn him against Hamlet, Ophelia appears, driven mad by her rejection by Hamlet and the death of her father.

Act IV, v (lines 164–97)

OPHELIA [*Sings.*] They bore him bare-fac'd on the bier,
And in his grave rain'd many a tear –
Fare you well, my dove.

LAERTES Hadst thou thy wits and didst persuade revenge,
It could not move thus.

OPHELIA You must sing *A-down a-down*, and you *Call him a-down-a*. O, how the wheel becomes it! It is the false steward that stole his master's daughter.

LAERTES This nothing's more than matter.

OPHELIA There's rosemary, that's for remembrance – pray you, love, remember. And there is pansies, that's for thoughts.

LAERTES A document in madness: thoughts and remembrance fitted.

OPHELIA There's fennel for you, and columbines. There's rue for you. And here's some for me. We may call it herb of grace a Sundays. You must wear your rue with a difference. There's a daisy. I would give you some violets, but they withered all when my father died. They say a made a good end.
[*Sings.*] For bonny sweet Robin is all my joy.

LAERTES Thought and affliction, passion, hell itself
She turns to favour and to prettiness.

OPHELIA [*Sings.*]
      And will 'a not come again?
      And will 'a not come again?
        No, no, he is dead,
        Go to thy death-bed,
      He never will come again.

      His beard was as white as snow,
        All flaxen was his poll.
        He is gone, he is gone,
        And we cast away moan.
        God a mercy on his soul.
And of all Christian souls. God buy you.

Hamlet has foiled the King's plan to have him killed on arrival in England, and returned to Denmark. The King has incited Laertes to challenge Hamlet to a duel. As they conspire against Hamlet, the Queen interrupts them with news of the death of Ophelia.

Act IV, vii (lines 166–83)

QUEEN There is a willow grows askant the brook
That shows his hoary leaves in the glassy stream.
Therewith fantastic garlands did she make
Of crow-flowers, nettles, daisies, and long purples,
That liberal shepherds give a grosser name,
But our cold maids do dead men's fingers call them.
There on the pendent boughs her crownet weeds
Clamb'ring to hang, an envious sliver broke,
When down her weedy trophies and herself
Fell in the weeping brook. Her clothes spread wide,
And mermaid-like awhile they bore her up,
Which time she chanted snatches of old lauds,
As one incapable of her own distress,
Or like a creature native and indued
Unto that element. But long it could not be
Till that her garments, heavy with their drink,
Pull'd the poor wretch from her melodious lay
To muddy death.

Hamlet and Horatio come across a gravedigger preparing Orphelia's grave.

Act V, i (lines 171–96)

GRAVEDIGGER Here's a skull now hath lien you i'th' earth three and twenty years.

HAMLET Whose was it?

GRAVEDIGGER A whoreson mad fellow's it was. Whose do you think it was?

HAMLET Nay, I know not.

GRAVEDIGGER A pestilence on him for a mad rogue! A poured a flagon of Rhenish on my head once. This same skull, sir, was Yorick's skull, the King's jester.

HAMLET This? [*Takes the skull.*]

GRAVEDIGGER E'en that.

HAMLET Alas, poor Yorick, I knew him, Horatio, a fellow of infinite jest, of most excellent fancy. He hath bore me on his back a thousand times, and now – how abhorred in my imagination it is. My gorge rises at it. Here hung those lips that I have kissed I know not how oft. Where be your gibes now, your gambols, your songs, your flashes of merriment, that were wont to set the table on a roar? Not one now to mock your own grinning? Quite chop-fallen? Now get you to my lady's chamber and tell her, let her paint an inch thick, to this favour she must come. Make her laugh at that. – Prithee, Horatio, tell me one thing.

HORATIO What's that, my lord?

HAMLET Dost thou think Alexander looked o' this fashion i'th' earth?

OTHELLO

Written and first performed about 1601–2

Iago is an ensign of Othello, a Moor serving as general for the state of Venice. Iago has been taking financial advantage of Roderigo, a gentleman of Venice who is in love with Desdemona. When Roderigo complains that Iago has been duping him, Iago denies it and tells him of his motives in serving Othello.

Act I, i (lines 40–64)

IAGO O sir, content you!
I follow him to serve my turn upon him.
We cannot all be masters, nor all masters
Cannot be truly followed. You shall mark
Many a duteous and knee-crooking knave
That, doting on his own obsequious bondage,
Wears out his time much like his master's ass
For nought but provender, and, when he's old, cashiered.
Whip me such honest knaves! Others there are
Who, trimmed in forms and visages of duty,
Keep yet their hearts attending on themselves
And, throwing but shows of service on their lords,
Do well thrive by them, and, when they have lined their coats,
Do themselves homage: these fellows have some soul
And such a one do I profess myself. For, sir,
It is as sure as you are Roderigo,
Were I the Moor, I would not be Iago.
In following him I follow but myself:
Heaven is my judge, not I for love and duty
But seeming so, for my peculiar end,
For when my outward action doth demonstrate
The native act and figure of my heart
In complement extern, 'tis not long after
But I will wear my heart upon my sleeve
For daws to peck at: I am not what I am.

Othello and Desdemona have married without telling her father
Brabantio, a Venetian Senator. Othello is taken to the Senate to
answer Brabantio's complaint that his daughter has been abducted.
The Duke of Venice and leader of the Senate asks Othello about
his courtship of Desdemona. Othello responds.

Act I, iii (lines 129–71)

OTHELLO Her father loved me, oft invited me,
Still questioned me the story of my life
From year to year – the battles, sieges, fortunes
That I have passed.
I ran it through, even from my boyish days
To th' very moment that he bade me tell it,
Wherein I spake of most disastrous chances,
Of moving accidents by flood and field,
Of hair-breadth scapes i'th' imminent deadly breach,
Of being taken by the insolent foe
And sold to slavery; of my redemption thence
And portance in my travailous history;
Wherein of antres vast and deserts idle,
Rough quarries, rocks and hills whose heads touch heaven
It was my hint to speak – such was my process –
And of the cannibals that each other eat,
The Anthropophagi, and men whose heads
Do grow beneath their shoulders. This to hear
Would Desdemona seriously incline,
But still the house affairs would draw her thence,
Which ever as she could with haste dispatch
She'd come again, and with a greedy ear
Devour up my discourse; which I, observing,
Took once a pliant hour and found good means
To draw from her a prayer of earnest heart
That I would all my pilgrimage dilate,
Whereof by parcels she had something heard
But not intentively. I did consent,
And often did beguile her of her tears
When I did speak of some distressful stroke

That my youth suffered. My story being done
She gave me for my pains a world of sighs,
She swore in faith 'twas strange, 'twas passing strange,
'Twas pitiful, 'twas wondrous pitiful;
She wished she had not heard it, yet she wished
That heaven had made her such a man. She thanked me
And bade me, if I had a friend that loved her,
I should but teach him how to tell my story
And that would woo her. Upon this hint I spake:
She loved me for the dangers I had passed
And I loved her that she did pity them.
This only is the witchcraft I have used:

Enter DESDEMONA, IAGO, *attendants.*

Here comes the lady, let her witness it.

Desdemona confirms her love for and commitment to Othello before the Senators.

Act I, iii (lines 250–61)

DESDEMONA That I did love the Moor to live with him
My downright violence and scorn of fortunes
May trumpet to the world. My heart's subdued
Even to the very quality of my lord:
I saw Othello's visage in his mind,
And to his honours and his valiant parts
Did I my soul and fortunes consecrate,
So that, dear lords, if I be left behind,
A moth of peace, and he go to the war,
The rites for which I love him are bereft me,
And I a heavy interim shall support
By his dear absence. Let me go with him.

Roderigo is disappointed at the loss of Desdemona. Iago consoles him that her love of Othello will not last, and encourages him to follow the couple to Cyprus.

Act I, iii (lines 321–48)

IAGO Virtue? a fig! 'tis in ourselves that we are thus, or thus. Our bodies are gardens, to the which our wills are gardeners. So that if we will plant nettles or sow lettuce, set hyssop and weed up thyme, supply it with one gender of herbs or distract it with many, either to have it sterile with idleness or manured with industry – why, the power and corrigible authority of this lies in our wills. If the balance of our lives had not one scale of reason to poise another of sensuality, the blood and baseness of our natures would conduct us to most preposterous conclusions. But we have reason to cool our raging motions, our carnal stings, our unbitted lusts; whereof I take this, that you call love, to be a sect or scion.

RODERIGO It cannot be.

IAGO It is merely a lust of the blood and a permission of the will. Come, be a man! Drown thyself? drown cats and blind puppies. I have professed me thy friend, and I confess me knit to thy deserving with cables of perdurable toughness. I could never better stead thee than now. Put money in thy purse.

*In Cyprus Iago has contrived a scuffle between Roderigo and
Othello's officer Michael Cassio, whom Iago resents. As a result
Cassio has lost favour with Othello and Desdemona has been
drawn into pleading his cause. Iago has used this to persuade Othello
that Desdemona has been unfaithful to him with Cassio. Othello
is gripped by jealousy.*

Act III, iii (lines 262–83)

OTHELLO This fellow's of exceeding honesty
And knows all qualities, with a learned spirit,
Of human dealings. If I do prove her haggard,
Though that her jesses were my dear heart-strings,
I'd whistle her off and let her down the wind
To prey at fortune. Haply for I am black
And have not those soft parts of conversation
That chamberers have, or for I am declined
Into the vale of years – yet that's not much –
She's gone, I am abused, and my relief
Must be to loathe her. O curse of marriage
That we can call these delicate creatures ours
And not their appetites! I had rather be a toad
And live upon the vapour of a dungeon
Than keep a corner in the thing I love
For others' uses. Yet 'tis the plague of great ones,
Prerogatived are they less than the base;
'Tis destiny unshunnable, like death –
Even then this forked plague is fated to us
When we do quicken.

Enter DESDEMONA *and* EMILIA.

Look where she comes:
If she be false, O then heaven mocks itself,
I'll not believe't.

Othello's jealousy grows.

Act III, iii (lines 333–60)

IAGO Look where he comes. Not poppy nor mandragora
Nor all the drowsy syrups of the world
Shall ever medicine thee to that sweet sleep
Which thou owedst yesterday.

OTHELLO Ha! Ha! false to me?

IAGO Why, how now, general? No more of that.

OTHELLO Avaunt, be gone, thou hast set me on the rack!
I swear 'tis better to be much abused
Than but to know't a little.

IAGO How now, my lord?

OTHELLO What sense had I of her stolen hours of lust?
I saw't not, thought it not, it harmed not me,
I slept the next night well, fed well, was free and merry;
I found not Cassio's kisses on her lips;
He that is robbed, not wanting what is stolen,
Let him not know't, and he's not robbed at all.

IAGO I am sorry to hear this.

OTHELLO I had been happy if the general camp,
Pioneers and all, had tasted her sweet body,
So I had nothing known. O now for ever
Farewell the tranquil mind, farewell content!
Farewell the plumed troops and the big wars
That makes ambition virtue! O farewell,
Farewell the neighing steed and the shrill trump,
The spirit-stirring drum, th'ear-piercing fife,
The royal banner, and all quality,
Pride, pomp and circumstance of glorious war!
And, O you mortal engines whose rude throats
Th'immortal Jove's dread clamours counterfeit,
Farewell: Othello's occupation's gone.

*Now convinced of Desdemona's faithlessness, Othello vows to take
revenge by killing Desdemona himself and having Iago kill Cassio.*

Act III, iii (lines 455–64)

IAGO Patience, I say, your mind perhaps may change.

OTHELLO Never, Iago. Like to the Pontic sea
Whose icy current and compulsive course
Ne'er keeps retiring ebb but keeps due on
To the Propontic and the Hellespont:
Even so my bloody thoughts with violent pace
Shall ne'er look back, ne'er ebb to humble love
Till that a capable and wide revenge
Swallow them up. Now by yond marble heaven
In the due reverence of a sacred vow
I here engage my words.

Believing Desdemona to be unfaithful, Othello has insulted her.
Now Desdemona sadly prepares for bed.

Act IV, iii (lines 16–58)

EMILIA Would you had never seen him!

DESDEMONA So would not I: my love doth so approve him
That even his stubbornness, his checks, his frowns
 – Prithee unpin me – have grace and favour.

EMILIA I have laid those sheets you bade me on the bed.

DESDEMONA All's one. Good faith, how foolish are our minds!
If I do die before thee, prithee shroud me
In one of these same sheets.

EMILIA Come, come, you talk.

DESDEMONA My mother had a maid called Barbary,
She was in love, and he she loved proved mad
And did forsake her. She had a song of 'willow',
An old thing 'twas, but it expressed her fortune
And she died singing it. That song tonight
Will not go from my mind. I have much to do
But to go hang my head all at one side
And sing it like poor Barbary. Prithee dispatch.

EMILIA Shall I go fetch your night-gown?

DESDEMONA No, unpin me here.

EMILIA This Lodovico is a proper man. A very handsome man.

DESDEMONA He speaks well.

EMILIA I know a lady in Venice would have walked barefoot to
Palestine for a touch of his nether lip.

DESDEMONA [*Sings.*]
> The poor soul sat sighing by a sycamore tree,
>> Sing all a green willow:
> Her hand on her bosom, her head on her knee,
>> Sing willow, willow, willow.
> The fresh streams ran by her and murmured her moans,
>> Sing willow, willow, willow:
> Her salt tears fell from her and softened the stones,
>> Sing willow, willow, willow.
> [*Speaks.*] Lay by these.
>> Willow, willow –
> [*Speaks.*] Prithee hie thee: he'll come anon.
> Sing all a green willow must be my garland.
> Let nobody blame him, his scorn I approve –
> [*Speaks.*] Nay, that's not next. Hark, who is't that
> knocks?

EMILIA It's the wind.

DESDEMONA [*Sings.*]
> I called my love false love; but what said he then?
>> Sing willow, willow, willow:
> If I court moe women, you'll couch with moe men.
> [*Speaks.*] So, get thee gone; good night. Mine eyes do itch,
> Doth that bode weeping?

Othello has come to the bedchamber to kill Desdemona.

Act V, ii (lines 1–22)

OTHELLO It is the cause, it is the cause, my soul!
Let me not name it to you, you chaste stars,
It is the cause. Yet I'll not shed her blood
Nor scar that whiter skin of hers than snow
And smooth as monumental alabaster:
Yet she must die, else she'll betray more men.
Put out the light, and then put out the light!
If I quench thee, thou flaming minister,
I can again thy former light restore
Should I repent me. But once put out thy light,
Thou cunning'st pattern of excelling nature,
I know not where is that Promethean heat
That can thy light relume: when I have plucked the rose
I cannot give it vital growth again,
It needs must wither. I'll smell thee on the tree;
O balmy breath, that dost almost persuade
Justice to break her sword! Once more, once more:
Be thus when thou art dead and I will kill thee
And love thee after. Once more, and that's the last.
[*He smells, then kisses her.*]
So sweet was ne'er so fatal. I must weep,
But they are cruel tears. This sorrow's heavenly,
It strikes where it doth love. She wakes.

*Emilia has found Desdemona dying and has raised the alarm.
She has also exposed Iago's falsehood. Now Othello prepares
to kill himself.*

Act V, ii (lines 259–81)

OTHELLO Behold, I have a weapon,
A better never did itself sustain
Upon a soldier's thigh. I have seen the day
That with this little arm and this good sword
I have made my way through more impediments
Than twenty times your stop: but, O vain boast,
Who can control his fate? 'Tis not so now.
Be not afraid, though you do see me weaponed:
Here is my journey's end, here is my butt
And very sea-mark of my utmost sail.
Do you go back dismayed? 'tis a lost fear:
Man but a rush against Othello's breast
And he retires. Where should Othello go?
Now: how dost thou look now? O ill-starred wench,
Pale as thy smock. When we shall meet at compt
This look of thine will hurl my soul from heaven
And fiends will snatch at it. Cold, cold, my girl,
Even like thy chastity. O cursed, cursed slave!
Whip me, ye devils,
From the possession of this heavenly sight!
Blow me about in winds, roast me in sulphur,
Wash me in steep-down gulfs of liquid fire!
O Desdemon! dead, Desdemon. Dead! O, O!

Othello makes his own obituary before killing himself.

Act V, ii (lines 338–59)

OTHELLO
Soft you, a word or two before you go.
I have done the state some service, and they know't:
No more of that. I pray you, in your letters,
When you shall these unlucky deeds relate,
Speak of me as I am. Nothing extenuate,
Nor set down aught in malice. Then must you speak
Of one that loved not wisely, but too well;
Of one not easily jealous, but, being wrought,
Perplexed in the extreme; of one whose hand,
Like the base Indian, threw a pearl away
Richer than all his tribe; of one whose subdued eyes,
Albeit unused to the melting mood,
Drops tears as fast as the Arabian trees
Their medicinable gum. Set you down this,
And say besides that in Aleppo once,
Where a malignant and a turbanned Turk
Beat a Venetian and traduced the state,
I took by th' throat the circumcised dog
And smote him – thus! [*He stabs himself.*]

LODOVICO O bloody period!

GRATIANO All that's spoke is marred.

OTHELLO I kissed thee ere I killed thee: no way but this,
Killing myself to die upon a kiss.

KING LEAR

Written and first performed in 1604–5

In his old age Lear, King of Britain, has decided to divide his kingdom between his three daughters, Goneril, Regan and Cordelia. Cordelia, Lear's youngest and favourite daughter, refuses to compete with her sisters for her share of the kingdom.

Act I, i (lines 89–108)

CORDELIA Nothing.

LEAR How, nothing will come of nothing. Speak again.

CORDELIA Unhappy that I am, I cannot heave
My heart into my mouth. I love your majesty
According to my bond, no more nor less.

LEAR How, how, Cordelia? Mend your speech a little,
Lest you may mar your fortunes.

CORDELIA Good my lord,
You have begot me, bred me, loved me. I
Return those duties back as are right fit,
Obey you, love you and most honour you.
Why have my sisters husbands, if they say
They love you all? Haply when I shall wed,
That lord whose hand must take my plight shall carry
Half my love with him, half my care and duty.
Sure I shall never marry like my sisters
To love my father all.

LEAR But goes thy heart with this?

CORDELIA Ay, my good lord.

LEAR So young and so untender?

CORDELIA So young, my lord, and true.

The Duke of Gloucester, one of the King's elderly attendants, has a son called Edgar, who is legitimate, and an illegitimate son called Edmund. Edmund has decided to trick Edgar out of his inheritance.

Act I, ii (lines 1–22)

EDMUND Thou, Nature, art my goddess; to thy law
My services are bound. Wherefore should I
Stand in the plague of custom, and permit
The curiosity of nations to deprive me?
For that I am some twelve or fourteen moonshines
Lag of a brother? Why bastard? Wherefore base?
When my dimensions are as well compact,
My mind as generous and my shape as true
As honest madam's issue? Why brand they us
With base? With baseness, bastardy? Base, base?
Who in the lusty stealth of nature take
More composition and fierce quality
Than doth within a dull stale tired bed
Go to the creating of a whole tribe of fops
Got 'tween a sleep and wake. Well, then,
Legitimate Edgar, I must have your land.
Our father's love is to the bastard Edmund
As to the legitimate. Fine word, 'legitimate'!
Well, my legitimate, if this letter speed
And my invention thrive, Edmund the base
Shall top the legitimate. I grow, I prosper:
Now gods, stand up for bastards!

Now owning half of the kingdom, Goneril has begun to reduce Lear's authority and retinue. Lear curses her.

Act I, iv (lines 267–81)

LEAR Hear, Nature, hear, dear goddess, hear:
Suspend thy purpose if thou didst intend
To make this creature fruitful.
Into her womb convey sterility,
Dry up in her the organs of increase,
And from her derogate body never spring
A babe to honour her. If she must teem,
Create her child of spleen, that it may live
And be a thwart disnatured torment to her.
Let it stamp wrinkles in her brow of youth,
With cadent tears fret channels in her cheeks,
Turn all her mother's pains and benefits
To laughter and contempt, that she may feel
How sharper than a serpent's tooth it is
To have a thankless child.

*Lear has come to Regan's house where he believes he will have a
better reception. Goneril has followed him, and she and her sister
progressively reduce Lear's allowance of attendants to none. As he
berates his daughters, Lear fears for his sanity. He goes out into the
stormy night.*

Act II, ii (lines 452–78)

GONERIL Hear me, my lord:
What need you five and twenty? Ten? Or five?
To follow in a house where twice so many
Have a command to tend you?

REGAN What need one?

LEAR O, reason not the need! Our basest beggars
Are in the poorest thing superfluous;
Allow not nature more than nature needs,
Man's life is cheap as beast's. Thou art a lady;
If only to go warm were gorgeous,
Why, nature needs not what thou gorgeous wear'st,
Which scarcely keeps thee warm. But for true need –
You heavens, give me that patience, patience I need!
You see me here, you gods, a poor old man,
As full of grief as age, wretched in both:
If it be you that stirs these daughters' hearts
Against their father, fool me not so much
To bear it tamely; touch me with noble anger,
And let not women's weapons, water-drops,
Stain my man's cheeks. No, you unnatural hags,
I will have such revenges on you both
That all the world shall – I will do such things –
What they are yet I know not, but they shall be
The terrors of the earth! You think I'll weep,
No, I'll not weep. [*Storm and tempest.*]
I have full cause of weeping, but this heart
Shall break into a hundred thousand flaws
Or e'er I'll weep. O fool, I shall go mad.

In the storm with his court jester, Lear calls upon the elements to do their worst.

Act III, ii (lines 1–24)

LEAR Blow winds and crack your cheeks! Rage, blow!
You cataracts and hurricanoes, spout
Till you have drenched our steeples, drowned the cocks!
You sulphurous and thought-executing fires,
Vaunt-couriers of oak-cleaving thunderbolts,
Singe my white head! And thou, all-shaking thunder,
Strike flat the thick rotundity o'the world,
Crack nature's moulds, all germens spill at once
That make ingrateful man!

FOOL O, nuncle, court holy-water in a dry house is better than this
rain-water out o'door. Good nuncle, in, and ask thy daughters
blessing. Here's a night pities neither wise men nor fools.

LEAR Rumble thy bellyful! Spit fire, spout rain!
Nor rain, wind, thunder, fire are my daughters;
I tax not you, you elements, with unkindness.
I never gave you kingdom, called you children;
You owe me no subscription. Why then, let fall
Your horrible pleasure. Here I stand your slave,
A poor, infirm, weak and despised old man.
But yet I call you servile ministers
That will with two pernicious daughters join
Your high-engendered battles 'gainst a head
So old and white as this. O ho! 'tis foul.

The Duke of Kent has found a rough shelter for Lear, who begins to develop sympathy for the people of his kingdom.

Act III, iv (lines 26–36)

LEAR [*To the Fool*] In boy, go first. You houseless poverty –
Nay, get thee in. I'll pray, and then I'll sleep.   *Exit Fool.*
[*Kneels.*] Poor naked wretches, wheresoe'er you are,
That bide the pelting of this pitiless storm,
How shall your houseless heads and unfed sides,
Your looped and windowed raggedness, defend you
From seasons such as these? O, I have ta'en
Too little care of this. Take physic, pomp,
Expose thyself to feel what wretches feel,
That thou mayst shake the superflux to them
And show the heavens more just.

After discovering his brother has falsely accused him of plotting against his father, Gloucester, Edgar has disguised himself as a mad beggar called Poor Tom and fled. Lear's encounter with him in the shelter marks the start of his madness.

Act III, iv (lines 83–108)

LEAR What hast thou been?

EDGAR A serving-man, proud in heart and mind, that curled my hair, wore gloves in my cap, served the lust of my mistress' heart and did the act of darkness with her; swore as many oaths as I spake words and broke them in the sweet face of heaven. One that slept in the contriving of lust and waked to do it. Wine loved I deeply, dice dearly; and, in woman, out-paramoured the Turk: false of heart, light of ear, bloody of hand; hog in sloth, fox in stealth, wolf in greediness, dog in madness, lion in prey. Let not the creaking of shoes, nor the rustling of silks, betray thy poor heart to woman. Keep thy foot out of brothels, thy hand out of plackets, thy pen from lenders' books, and defy the foul fiend. Still through the hawthorn blows the cold wind, says suum, mun, nonny, Dauphin my boy, my boy, *cessez!* Let him trot by. [*Storm still.*]

LEAR Why, thou wert better in a grave than to answer with thy uncovered body this extremity of the skies. Is man no more than this? Consider him well. Thou ow'st the worm no silk, the beast no hide, the sheep no wool, the cat no perfume. Ha? Here's three on's us are sophisticated; thou art the thing itself. Unaccommodated man is no more but such a poor, bare, forked animal as thou art. Off, off, you lendings: come, unbutton here.

Against the instructions of Regan and the Duke of Cornwall,
Gloucester has tried to help Lear. He is captured and has his eyes
put out, during which a servant in his revulsion mortally wounds
Cornwall and in turn is killed by Regan.

Act III, vii (lines 53–93)

GLOUCESTER I am tied to the stake and I must stand the course.

REGAN Wherefore to Dover, sir?

GLOUCESTER Because I would not see thy cruel nails
Pluck out his poor old eyes; nor thy fierce sister
In his anointed flesh stick boarish fangs.
The sea, with such a storm as his bare head
In hell-bent night endured, would have buoyed up
And quenched the stelled fires.
Yet, poor old heart, he holp the heavens to rain.
If wolves had at thy gate howled that stern time,
Thou shouldst have said, 'Good porter, turn the key,
All cruels else subscribed'; but I shall see
The winged vengeance overtake such children.

CORNWALL See't shalt thou never. Fellows, hold the chair;
Upon these eyes of thine I'll set my foot.

GLOUCESTER He that will think to live till he be old,
Give me some help! – O cruel! O you gods!

REGAN One side will mock another – th'other too.

CORNWALL If you see vengeance –

1 SERVANT Hold your hand, my lord.
I have served you ever since I was a child,
But better service have I never done you
Than now to bid you hold.

REGAN How now, you dog?

1 SERVANT If you did wear a beard upon your chin,
I'd shake it on this quarrel. What do you mean?

CORNWALL My villein? [*They draw and fight.*]

1 SERVANT Nay then, come on, and take the chance of anger.
[*He wounds Cornwall.*]

REGAN [*to another Servant*]
Give me thy sword. A peasant stand up thus?
[*She takes a sword and runs at him behind. Kills him.*]

1 SERVANT O, I am slain. My lord, you have one eye left
To see some mischief on him. O! [*He dies.*]

CORNWALL Lest it see more, prevent it. Out, vile jelly,
Where is thy lustre now?

GLOUCESTER All dark and comfortless? Where's my son Edmund?
Edmund, enkindle all the sparks of nature
To quit this horrid act.

REGAN Out, treacherous villain,
Thou call'st on him that hates thee. It was he
That made the overture of thy treasons to us,
Who is too good to pity thee.

GLOUCESTER O my follies! Then Edgar was abused?
Kind gods, forgive me that and prosper him.

REGAN [*to a Servant*]
Go, thrust him out at gates and let him smell
His way to Dover.

The Duke of Albany is appalled by his wife's deeds towards her father.

Act IV, ii (lines 29–51)

GONERIL I have been worth the whistling.

ALBANY O Goneril,
You are not worth the dust which the rude wind
Blows in your face. I fear your disposition;
That nature which contemns its origin
Cannot be bordered certain in itself.
She that herself will sliver and disbranch
From her material sap perforce must wither,
And come to deadly use.

GONERIL No more, the text is foolish.

ALBANY Wisdom and goodness to the vile seem vile;
Filths savour but themselves. What have you done?
Tigers, not daughters, what have you performed?
A father, and a gracious aged man
Whose reverence even the head-lugged bear would lick,
Most barbarous, most degenerate, have you madded.
Could my good brother suffer you to do it?
A man, a prince, by him so benefitted?
If that the heavens do not their visible spirits
Send quickly down to tame these vile offences,
It will come:
Humanity must perforce prey on itself,
Like monsters of the deep.

*Gloucester has been befriended by his son Edgar, still in disguise.
At his father's request he has taken him to Dover where Gloucester
wishes to cast himself from the cliff. Edgar enacts the fall in order to
bring his father to a new state of mind.*

Act IV, vi (lines 11–77)

EDGAR Come on, sir, here's the place. Stand still: how fearful
And dizzy 'tis to cast one's eyes so low.
The crows and choughs that wing the midway air
Show scarce so gross as beetles. Half-way down
Hangs one that gathers samphire, dreadful trade;
Methinks he seems no bigger than his head.
The fishermen that walk upon the beach
Appear like mice, and yon tall anchoring barque
Diminished to her cock, her cock a buoy
Almost too small for sight. The murmuring surge
That on th'unnumbered idle pebble chafes,
Cannot be heard so high. I'll look no more,
Lest my brain turn and the deficient sight
Topple down headlong.

GLOUCESTER Set me where you stand.

EDGAR Give me your hand: you are now within a foot
Of th'extreme verge. For all beneath the moon
Would I not leap upright.

GLOUCESTER Let go my hand.
Here, friend, 's another purse, in it a jewel
Well worth a poor man's taking.
Fairies and gods
Prosper it with thee. Go thou further off;
Bid me farewell and let me hear thee going.

EDGAR Now fare ye well, good sir.

GLOUCESTER With all my heart.

EDGAR [*aside*] Why I do trifle thus with his despair
Is done to cure it.

GLOUCESTER [*He kneels.*] O you mighty gods,
This world I do renounce and in your sights
Shake patiently my great affliction off.
If I could bear it longer and not fall
To quarrel with your great opposeless wills,
My snuff and loathed part of nature should
Burn itself out. If Edgar live, O, bless him!
Now, fellow, fare thee well. [*He falls.*]

EDGAR Gone, sir; farewell.
[*aside*] And yet I know not how conceit may rob
The treasury of life when life itself
Yields to the theft. Had he been where he thought,
By this had thought been past.
[*to Gloucester*] Alive or dead?
Ho, you, sir! Friend, hear you, sir? Speak! –
[*aside*] Thus might he pass indeed. Yet he revives. –
What are you, sir?

GLOUCESTER Away and let me die.

EDGAR Hadst thou been aught but gossamer, feathers, air,
So many fathom down precipitating,
Thou'dst shivered like an egg; but thou dost breathe,
Hast heavy substance, bleed'st not, speak'st, art sound.
Ten masts at each make not the altitude
Which thou hast perpendicularly fell.
Thy life's a miracle. Speak yet again.

GLOUCESTER But have I fallen, or no?

EDGAR From the dread summit of this chalky bourn.
Look up a-height: the shrill-gorged lark so far
Cannot be seen or heard. Do but look up.

GLOUCESTER Alack, I have no eyes.
Is wretchedness deprived that benefit
To end itself by death? 'Twas yet some comfort
When misery could beguile the tyrant's rage
And frustrate his proud will.

EDGAR Give me your arm.
Up, so. How is't? Feel you your legs? You stand.

GLOUCESTER Too well, too well.

EDGAR This is above all strangeness.
Upon the crown o'the cliff what thing was that
Which parted from you?

GLOUCESTER A poor unfortunate beggar.

EDGAR As I stood here below methought his eyes
Were two full moons. He had a thousand noses,
Horns whelked and waved like the enraged sea.
It was some fiend. Therefore, thou happy father,
Think that the clearest gods, who make them honours
Of men's impossibilities, have preserved thee.

GLOUCESTER I do remember now. Henceforth I'll bear
Affliction till it do cry out itself
'Enough, enough' and die.

Gloucester and Lear meet again.

Act IV, vi (lines 105–83)

GLOUCESTER The trick of that voice I do well remember:
Is't not the King?

LEAR Ay, every inch a king.
When I do stare, see how the subject quakes.
I pardon that man's life. What was thy cause?
Adultery?
Thou shalt not die – die for adultery? No!
The wren goes to't and the small gilded fly
Does lecher in my sight. Let copulation thrive,
For Gloucester's bastard son was kinder to his father
Than were my daughters got 'tween the lawful sheets.
To't, luxury, pell-mell, for I lack soldiers.
Behold yon simp'ring dame,
Whose face between her forks presages snow,
That minces virtue and does shake the head
To hear of pleasure's name –
The fitchew, nor the soiled horse, goes to't with a more riotous
appetite. Down from the waist they are centaurs, though women
all above. But to the girdle do the gods inherit, beneath is all the
fiend's: there's hell, there's darkness, there is the sulphurous pit,
burning, scalding, stench, consumption! Fie, fie, fie! Pah, pah!
Give me an ounce of civet, good apothecary, to sweeten my
imagination. There's money for thee.

GLOUCESTER O, let me kiss that hand!

LEAR Let me wipe it first, it smells of mortality.

GLOUCESTER O ruined piece of nature, this great world
Shall so wear out to naught. Dost thou know me?

LEAR I remember thine eyes well enough. Dost thou squiny at
me?
No, do thy worst, blind Cupid, I'll not love.
Read thou this challenge, mark but the penning of it.

GLOUCESTER Were all thy letters suns, I could not see one.

EDGAR [*aside*] I would not take this from report: it is,
And my heart breaks at it.

LEAR Read.

GLOUCESTER What? With the case of eyes?

LEAR Oh ho, are you there with me? No eyes in your head,
nor no money in your purse? Your eyes are in a heavy case,
your purse in a light, yet you see how this world goes.

GLOUCESTER I see it feelingly.

LEAR What, art mad? A man may see how this world goes
with no eyes. Look with thine ears. See how yon justice rails
upon yon simple thief. Hark in thine ear: change places and
handy-dandy, which is the justice, which is the thief? Thou
hast seen a farmer's dog bark at a beggar?

GLOUCESTER Ay, sir.

LEAR And the creature run from the cur – there thou mightst
behold the great image of authority: a dog's obeyed in office.
Thou, rascal beadle, hold thy bloody hand;
Why dost thou lash that whore? Strip thine own back,
Thou hotly lusts to use her in that kind
For which thou whipp'st her. The usurer hangs the cozener.
Through tattered clothes great vices do appear;
Robes and furred gowns hide all. Plate sin with gold,
And the strong lance of justice hurtless breaks;
Arm it in rags, a pigmy's straw does pierce it.
None does offend, none, I say none. I'll able 'em;
Take that of me, my friend, who have the power
To seal th'accuser's lips. Get thee glass eyes,
And like a scurvy politician seem
To see the things thou dost not. Now, now, now, now, pull
off my boots; harder, harder, so.

EDGAR [*aside*] O matter and impertinency mixed,
Reason in madness.

LEAR If thou wilt weep my fortunes, take my eyes.
I know thee well enough, thy name is Gloucester.
Thou must be patient. We came crying hither:
Thou knowst the first time that we smell the air
We wawl and cry. I will preach to thee: mark me.

GLOUCESTER Alack, alack the day!

LEAR When we are born we cry that we are come
To this great stage of fools. This a good block:
It were a delicate stratagem to shoe
A troop of horse with felt. I'll put it in proof
And when I have stolen upon these son-in-laws,
Then kill, kill, kill, kill, kill, kill!

*Cordelia has returned to Britain with an army to seek out Lear.
Having found him deranged, she and her attendants have restored
him to sanity. Lear seeks her forgiveness.*

Act IV, vii (lines 45–70)

CORDELIA How does my royal lord? How fares your majesty?

LEAR You do me wrong to take me out o'the grave.
Thou art a soul in bliss, but I am bound
Upon a wheel of fire that mine own tears
Do scald like molten lead.

CORDELIA Sir, do you know me?

LEAR You are a spirit, I know; where did you die?

CORDELIA Still, still far wide.

GENTLEMAN He's scarce awake; let him alone awhile.

LEAR Where have I been? Where am I? Fair daylight?
I am mightily abused. I should ev'n die with pity
To see another thus. I know not what to say.
I will not swear these are my hands: let's see –
I feel this pinprick. Would I were assured
Of my condition.

CORDELIA [*Kneels.*] O look upon me, sir,
And hold your hands in benediction o'er me!
[*She restrains him as he tries to kneel.*]
No, sir, you must not kneel.

LEAR Pray do not mock me.
I am a very foolish, fond old man,
Fourscore and upward, not an hour more or less;
And to deal plainly,
I fear I am not in my perfect mind.
Methinks I should know you and know this man,
Yet I am doubtful; for I am mainly ignorant
What place this is and all the skill I have
Remembers not these garments; nor I know not

121

Where I did lodge last night. Do not laugh at me,
For, as I am a man, I think this lady
To be my child Cordelia.

CORDELIA And so I am, I am.

Having been defeated in battle by the armies of Goneril and Regan, Cordelia and Lear are captured by Edmund, who has been assisting the two sisters. He sends them to prison with secret orders to kill them.

Act V, iii (lines 3–26)

CORDELIA We are not the first
Who with best meaning have incurred the worst.
For thee, oppressed King, I am cast down;
Myself could else outfrown false fortune's frown.
Shall we not see these daughters and these sisters?

LEAR No, no, no, no. Come, let's away to prison;
We two alone will sing like birds i'the cage.
When thou dost ask me blessing I'll kneel down
And ask of thee forgiveness. So we'll live
And pray and sing, and tell old tales, and laugh
At gilded butterflies, and hear poor rogues
Talk of court news; and we'll talk with them too –
Who loses and who wins, who's in, who's out –
And take upon's the mystery of things
As if we were God's spies. And we'll wear out
In a walled prison packs and sects of great ones
That ebb and flow by the moon.

EDMUND [*to soldiers*] Take them away.

LEAR Upon such sacrifices, my Cordelia,
The gods themselves throw incense. Have I caught thee?
[*Embraces her.*]
He that parts us shall bring a brand from heaven,
And fire us hence like foxes. Wipe thine eyes;
The good years shall devour them, flesh and fell,
Ere they shall make us weep!
We'll see 'em starved first: come.

Lear has found Cordelia as she is being hanged. He tries to restore her to life.

Act V, iii (lines 255–73)

LEAR Howl, howl, howl, howl! O, you are men of stones!
Had I your tongues and eyes, I'd use them so
That heaven's vault should crack: she's gone for ever.
I know when one is dead and when one lives;
She's dead as earth. [*He lays her down.*]
Lend me a looking-glass;
If that her breath will mist or stain the stone,
Why then she lives.

KENT Is this the promised end?

EDGAR Or image of that horror?

ALBANY Fall, and cease.

LEAR This feather stirs, she lives: if it be so,
It is a chance which does redeem all sorrows
That ever I have felt.

KENT O, my good master!

LEAR Prithee, away!

EDGAR 'Tis noble Kent, your friend.

LEAR A plague upon you murderers, traitors all;
I might have saved her; now she's gone for ever.
Cordelia, Cordelia, stay a little. Ha?
What is't thou sayst? Her voice was ever soft,
Gentle and low, an excellent thing in woman.
I killed the slave that was a-hanging thee.

Lear dies as he searches for signs of life in Cordelia.

Act V, iii (lines 304–25)

LEAR And my poor fool is hanged. No, no, no life!
Why should a dog, a horse, a rat have life
And thou no breath at all? O thou'lt come no more,
Never, never, never, never, never.
[*to Edgar*] Pray you undo this button. Thank you, sir. O, o, o, o.
Do you see this? Look on her: look, her lips,
Look there, look there! [*He dies.*]

EDGAR He faints: my lord, my lord!

KENT Break, heart, I prithee break.

EDGAR Look up, my lord.

KENT Vex not his ghost; O, let him pass. He hates him
That would upon the rack of this tough world
Stretch him out longer.

EDGAR O he is gone indeed.

KENT The wonder is he hath endured so long;
He but usurped his life.

ALBANY Bear them from hence. Our present business
Is to general woe.
[*to Edgar and Kent*] Friends of my soul, you twain,
Rule in this realm and the gored state sustain.

KENT I have a journey, sir, shortly to go;
My master calls me, I must not say no.

EDGAR The weight of this sad time we must obey,
Speak what we feel, not what we ought to say.
The oldest hath borne most; we that are young
Shall never see so much, nor live so long.

MACBETH

Written and first performed in 1606

The King of Norway, aided by some Scottish lords, has invaded Scotland, but he has been defeated by the army of Duncan, King of Scotland. Macbeth, Thane of Glamis and one of Duncan's generals, has distinguished himself in battle. Three witches wait to accost Macbeth as he returns from the battlefield with his fellow general Banquo.

Act I, iii (lines 1–37)

1 WITCH Where hast thou been, Sister?

2 WITCH Killing swine.

3 WITCH Sister, where thou?

1 WITCH A sailor's wife had chestnuts in her lap,
And mounch'd, and mounch'd, and mounch'd: 'Give me,' quoth I: –
'Aroynt thee, witch!'; the rump-fed ronyon cries.
Her husband's to Aleppo gone, master o'th' *Tiger*:
But in a sieve I'll thither sail,
And like a rat without a tail;
I'll do, I'll do, and I'll do.

2 WITCH I'll give thee a wind.

1 WITCH Th'art kind.

3 WITCH And I another.

1 WITCH I myself have all the other;
And the very ports they blow,
All the quarters that they know
I'th' shipman's card.

I'll drain him dry as hay:
Sleep shall neither night nor day
Hang upon his penthouse lid;
He shall live a man forbid.
Weary sev'n-nights nine times nine,
Shall he dwindle, peak, and pine:
Though his bark cannot be lost,
Yet it shall be tempest-tost.
Look what I have.

2 WITCH Show me, show me.

1 WITCH Here I have a pilot's thumb,
Wrack'd, as homeward he did come. [*Drum within.*]

3 WITCH A drum! a drum!
Macbeth doth come.

ALL The Weird Sisters, hand in hand,
Posters of the sea and land,
Thus do go about, about:
Thrice to thine, and thrice to mine,
And thrice again, to make up nine
Peace! – the charm's wound up.

The Thane of Cawdor, whom Duncan had believed to be totally trustworthy, sided with the King of Norway. Duncan's son Malcolm describes his execution.

Act I, iv (lines 1–13)

DUNCAN Is execution done on Cawdor? Or not
Those in commission yet return'd?

MALCOLM My Liege,
They are not yet come back; but I have spoke
With one that saw him die: who did report,
That very frankly he confess'd his treasons,
Implor'd your Highness' pardon, and set forth
A deep repentance. Nothing in his life
Became him like the leaving it: he died
As one that had been studied in his death,
To throw away the dearest thing he ow'd,
As 'twere a careless trifle.

DUNCAN There's no art
To find the mind's construction in the face:
He was a gentleman on whom I built
An absolute trust –

Macbeth has written to his wife to tell her of his meeting with the witches, of his new honour, and of the witches' prophesy that he will be King of Scotland. On hearing that Duncan is to come to their castle overnight, Lady Macbeth resolves that he shall be murdered.

Act I, v (lines 37–53)

LADY MACBETH The raven himself is hoarse,
That croaks the fatal entrance of Duncan
Under my battlements. Come, you Spirits
That tend on mortal thoughts, unsex me here,
And fill me, from the crown to the toe, top-full
Of direst cruelty! make thick my blood,
Stop up th'access and passage to remorse;
That no compunctious visitings of Nature
Shake my fell purpose, nor keep pace between
Th'effect and it! Come to my woman's breasts,
And take my milk for gall, you murth'ring ministers,
Wherever in your sightless substances
You wait on Nature's mischief! Come, thick Night,
And pall thee in the dunnest smoke of Hell,
That my keen knife see not the wound it makes,
Nor Heaven peep through the blanket of the dark,
To cry, 'Hold, Hold!'

Having committed himself to murder Duncan, Macbeth is horrified by the significance of such an act.

Act I, vii (lines 1–28)

MACBETH If it were done, when 'tis done, then 'twere well
It were done quickly: if th'assassination
Could trammel up the consequence, and catch
With his surcease success; that but this blow
Might be the be-all and the end-all – here,
But here, upon this bank and shoal of time,
We'd jump the life to come. – But in these cases,
We still have judgment here; that we but teach
Bloody instructions, which, being taught, return
To plague th'inventor: this even-handed Justice
Commends th'ingredience of our poison'd chalice
To our own lips. He's here in double trust:
First, as I am his kinsman and his subject,
Strong both against the deed; then, as his host,
Who should against his murtherer shut the door,
Not bear the knife myself. Besides, this Duncan
Hath borne his faculties so meek, hath been
So clear in his great office, that his virtues
Will plead like angels, trumpet-tongu'd, against
The deep damnation of his taking-off;
And Pity, like a naked new-born babe,
Striding the blast, or heaven's Cherubins, hors'd
Upon the sightless couriers of the air,
Shall blow the horrid deed in every eye,
That tears shall drown the wind. – I have no spur
To prick the sides of my intent, but only
Vaulting ambition, which o'erleaps itself
And falls on th'other –

Macbeth prepares to murder Duncan.

Act II, i (lines 33–64)

MACBETH Is this a dagger, which I see before me,
The handle toward my hand? Come, let me clutch thee: –
I have thee not, and yet I see thee still.
Art thou not, fatal vision, sensible
To feeling, as to sight? or art thou but
A dagger of the mind, a false creation,
Proceeding from the heat-oppressed brain?
I see thee yet, in form as palpable
As this which now I draw.
Thou marshall'st me the way that I was going;
And such an instrument I was to use. –
Mine eyes are made the fools o'th' other senses,
Or else worth all the rest: I see thee still;
And on thy blade, and dudgeon, gouts of blood,
Which was not so before. – There's no such thing.
It is the bloody business which informs
Thus to mine eyes. – Now o'er the one half-world
Nature seems dead, and wicked dreams abuse
The curtain'd sleep: Witchcraft celebrates
Pale Hecate's off'rings; and wither'd Murther,
Alarum'd by his sentinel, the wolf,
Whose howl's his watch, thus with his stealthy pace,
With Tarquin's ravishing strides, towards his design
Moves like a ghost. – Thou sure and firm-set earth,
Hear not my steps, which way they walk, for fear
Thy very stones prate of my where-about,
And take the present horror from the time,
Which now suits with it. – Whiles I threat, he lives:
Words to the heat of deeds too cold breath gives.
[*A bell rings.*]
I go, and it is done: the bell invites me.
Hear it not, Duncan; for it is a knell
That summons thee to Heaven, or to Hell.

Macbeth has killed Duncan, and is in deep remorse. Lady Macbeth chides him and takes command of the situation.

Act II, ii (lines 20–72)

MACBETH This is a sorry sight.

LADY MACBETH A foolish thought to say a sorry sight.

MACBETH There's one did laugh in's sleep, and one cried, 'Murther!'
That they did wake each other: I stood and heard them;
But they did say their prayers, and address'd them
Again to sleep.

LADY MACBETH There are two lodg'd together.

MACBETH One cried, 'God bless us!' and, 'Amen,' the other,
As they had seen me with these hangman's hands.
List'ning their fear, I could not say, 'Amen,'
When they did say, 'God bless us.'

LADY MACBETH Consider it not so deeply.

MACBETH But wherefore could not I pronounce 'Amen'?
I had most need of blessing, and 'Amen'
Stuck in my throat.

LADY MACBETH These deeds must not be thought
After these ways: so, it will make us mad.

MACBETH Methought, I heard a voice cry, 'Sleep no more!
Macbeth does murther Sleep,' – the innocent Sleep;
Sleep, that knits up the ravell'd sleave of care.
The death of each day's life, sore labour's bath.
Balm of hurt minds, great Nature's second course.
Chief nourisher in life's feast; –

LADY MACBETH What do you mean?

MACBETH Still it cried, 'Sleep no more!' to all the house:
'Glamis hath murther'd Sleep, and therefore Cawdor
Shall sleep no more, Macbeth shall sleep no more!'

LADY MACBETH Who was it that thus cried? Why, worthy Thane,

You do unbend your noble strength, to think
So brainsickly of things. Go, get some water.
And wash this filthy witness from your hand. –
Why did you bring these daggers from the place?
They must lie there: go, carry them, and smear
The sleepy grooms with blood.

MACBETH I'll go no more:
I am afraid to think what I have done;
Look on't again I dare not.

LADY MACBETH Infirm of purpose!
Give me the daggers. The sleeping, and the dead,
Are but as pictures; 'tis the eye of childhood
That fears a painted devil. If he do bleed,
I'll gild the faces of the grooms withal,
For it must seem their guilt. *Exit.*
[*Knocking within.*]

MACBETH Whence is that knocking? –
How is't with me, when every noise appals me?
What hands are here? Ha! they pluck out mine eyes.
Will all great Neptune's ocean wash this blood
Clean from my hand? No, this my hand will rather
The multitudinous seas incarnadine,
Making the green one red.
        Re-enter LADY MACBETH.

LADY MACBETH My hands are of your colour; but I shame
To wear a heart so white. [*knock*] I hear a knocking
At the south entry: – retire we to our chamber.
A little water clears us of this deed:
How easy is it then! Your constancy
Hath left you unattended. –
[*knock*] Hark! more knocking.
Get on your night-gown, lest occasion call us,
And show us to be watchers. – Be not lost
So poorly in your thoughts.

MACBETH To know my deed, 'twere best not know myself.
[*knock*] Wake Duncan with thy knocking: I would thou couldst!

Macbeth has just had Banquo killed. During the feast immediately afterwards Macbeth sees his ghost.

Act III, iv (lines 49–82)

MACBETH Thou canst not say, I did it: never shake
Thy glory locks at me.

ROSSE Gentlemen, rise; his Highness is not well.

LADY MACBETH Sit, worthy friends. My Lord is often thus,
And hath been from his youth: pray you, keep seat;
The fit is momentary; upon a thought
He will again be well. If much you note him,
You shall offend him, and extend his passion;
Feed, and regard him not. – Are you a man?

MACBETH Ay, and a bold one, that dare look on that
Which might appal the Devil.

LADY MACBETH O proper stuff!
This is the very painting of your fear:
This is the air-drawn dagger, which, you said,
Led you to Duncan. O! these flaws and starts
(Impostors to true fear), would well become
A woman's story at a winter's fire,
Authoris'd by her grandam. Shame itself!
Why do you make such faces? When all's done,
You look but on a stool.

MACBETH Pr'ythee, see there!
Behold! look! lo! how say you?
Why, what care I? If thou canst nod, speak too. –
If charnel-houses and our graves must send
Those that we bury, back, our monuments
Shall be the maws of kites. [*Ghost disappears.*]

LADY MACBETH What! quite unmann'd in folly?

MACBETH If I stand here, I saw him.

LADY MACBETH Fie! for shame!

MACBETH Blood hath been shed ere now, i'th' olden time,
Ere humane statute purg'd the gentle weal;
Ay, and since too, murthers have been perform'd
Too terrible for the ear: the time has been,
That, when the brains were out, the man would die,
And there an end; but now, they rise again,
With twenty mortal murthers on their crowns,
And push us from our stools. This is more strange
Than such a murther is.

Lady Macbeth has become deranged. The doctor and an attendant watch her sleepwalking.

Act V, i (lines 36–70)

LADY MACBETH Out, damned spot! out, I say! – One; two: why, then 'tis time to do't. – Hell is murky. – Fie, my Lord, fie! a soldier, and afeard? – What need we fear who knows it, when none can call our power to accompt? – Yet who would have thought the old man to have had so much blood in him?

DOCTOR Do you mark that?

LADY MACBETH The Thane of Fife had a wife: where is she now? – What, will these hands ne'er be clean? – No more o'that, my Lord, no more o'that: you mar all with this starting.

DOCTOR Go to, go to: you have known what you should not.

GENTLEWOMAN She has spoke what she should not, I am sure of that: Heaven knows what she has known.

LADY MACBETH Here's the smell of the blood still: all the perfumes of Arabia will not sweeten this little hand. Oh! oh! oh!

DOCTOR What a sigh is there! The heart is sorely charg'd.

GENTLEWOMAN I would not have such a heart in my bosom, for the dignity of the whole body.

DOCTOR Well, well, well.

GENTLEWOMAN Pray God it be, sir.

DOCTOR This disease is beyond my practice: yet I have known those which have walk'd in their sleep, who have died holily in their beds.

LADY MACBETH Wash your hands, put on your night-gown; look not so pale. – I tell you yet again, Banquo's buried: he cannot come out on's grave.

DOCTOR Even so?

LADY MACBETH To bed, to bed: there's knocking at the gate. Come, come, come, come, give me your hand. What's done cannot be undone. To bed, to bed, to bed.

Macbeth hears the news that his wife has died.

Act V, v (lines 7–28)

MACBETH What is that noise?
[*a cry within, of women*]

SEYTON It is the cry of women, my good Lord. *Exit.*

MACBETH I have almost forgot the taste of fears.
The time has been, my senses would have cool'd
To hear a night-shriek; and my fell of hair
Would at a dismal treatise rouse, and stir,
As life were in't. I have supp'd full with horrors:
Direness, familiar to my slaughterous thoughts,
Cannot once start me.

Re-enter SEYTON.

Wherefore was that cry?

SEYTON The Queen, my Lord, is dead.

MACBETH She should have died hereafter:
There would have been a time for such a word. –
To-morrow, and to-morrow, and to-morrow,
Creeps in this petty pace from day to day,
To the last syllable of recorded time;
And all our yesterdays have lighted fools
The way to dusty death. Out, out, brief candle!
Life's but a walking shadow; a poor player,
That struts and frets his hour upon the stage,
And then is heard no more: it is a tale
Told by an idiot, full of sound and fury,
Signifying nothing.

ANTONY AND CLEOPATRA

Written and first performed in 1606

Mark Antony, Octavius Caesar and Lepidus are the joint rulers (triumvirs) of the Roman Empire. However, Antony has been drawn away from affairs of state to Egypt and its queen Cleopatra. In Egypt Cleopatra accuses Antony of being the pawn of his wife Fulvia and of Octavius Caesar. Antony reacts to her taunts.

Act I, i (lines 34–56)

ANTONY Let Rome in Tiber melt, and the wide arch
Of the ranged empire fall! Here is my space!
Kingdoms are clay! Our dungy earth alike
Feeds beast as man. The nobleness of life
Is to do thus, when such a mutual pair
And such a twain can do't, in which I bind,
On pain of punishment, the world to weet
We stand up peerless.

CLEOPATRA Excellent falsehood!
Why did he marry Fulvia and not love her?
I'll seem the fool I am not. Antony
Will be himself.

ANTONY But stirred by Cleopatra.
Now, for the love of Love and her soft hours,
Let's not confound the time with conference harsh.
There's not a minute of our lives should stretch
Without some pleasure now. What sport tonight?

CLEOPATRA Hear the ambassadors.

ANTONY Fie, wrangling queen,
Whom everything becomes – to chide, to laugh,
To weep; whose every passion fully strives
To make itself, in thee, fair and admired!
No messenger but thine, and all alone
Tonight we'll wander through the streets and note
The qualities of people. Come, my queen!
Last night you did desire it. [*to the Messenger*] Speak not to us.

139

On hearing the news of the death of his wife Fulvia, Antony resolves to leave Egypt and Cleopatra. He tells his most trusted follower Enobarbus of his decision.

Act I, ii (lines 127–60)

ANTONY There's a great spirit gone! Thus did I desire it.
What our contempts doth often hurl from us
We wish it ours again. The present pleasure,
By revolution lowering, does become
The opposite of itself. She's good, being gone.
The hand could pluck her back that shoved her on.
I must from this enchanting queen break off.
Ten thousand harms, more than the ills l know,
My idleness doth hatch. How now, Enobarbus!

Enter ENOBARBUS.

ENOBARBUS What's your pleasure, sir?

ANTONY I must with haste from hence.

ENOBARBUS Why then we kill all our women. We see how mortal an unkindness is to them. If they suffer our departure, death's the word.

ANTONY I must be gone.

ENOBARBUS Under a compelling occasion let women die. It were pity to cast them away for nothing, though between them and a great cause they should be esteemed nothing. Cleopatra, catching but the least noise of this, dies instantly. I have seen her die twenty times upon far poorer moment. I do think there is mettle in death which commits some loving act upon her, she hath such a celerity in dying.

ANTONY She is cunning past man's thought.

ENOBARBUS Alack, sir, no; her passions are made of nothing but the finest part of pure love. We cannot call her winds and waters sighs and tears; they are greater storms and tempests than almanacs can report. This cannot be cunning in her. If it be, she makes a shower of rain as well as Jove.

ANTONY Would I had never seen her!

ENOBARBUS O, sir, you had then left unseen a wonderful piece of work, which not to have been blest withal would have discredited your travel.

In Rome, Caesar criticises Antony for staying in Egypt and neglecting affairs of state.

Act I, iv (lines 16–33)

CAESAR You are too indulgent. Let's grant it is not
Amiss to tumble on the bed of Ptolemy,
To give a kingdom for a mirth, to sit
And keep the turn of tippling with a slave,
To reel the streets at noon, and stand the buffet
With knaves that smell of sweat. Say this becomes him –
As his composure must be rare indeed
Whom these things cannot blemish – yet must Antony
No way excuse his foils, when we do bear
So great weight in his lightness. If he filled
His vacancy with his voluptuousness,
Full surfeits and the dryness of his bones
Call on him for't. But to confound such time
That drums him from his sport, and speaks as loud
As his own state and ours, 'tis to be chid
As we rate boys who, being mature in knowledge,
Pawn their experience to their present pleasure
And so rebel to judgment.

In Egypt, Cleopatra is missing the departed Antony and recollecting her past loves, Julius Caesar and Pompey.

Act I, v (lines 19–35)

CLEOPATRA O, Charmian,
Where think'st thou he is now? Stands he, or sits he?
Or does he walk? Or is he on his horse?
O happy horse, to bear the weight of Antony!
Do bravely, horse, for wot'st thou whom thou mov'st?
The demi-Atlas of this earth, the arm
And burgonet of men! He's speaking now,
Or murmuring 'Where's my serpent of old Nile?'
For so he calls me. Now I feed myself
With most delicious poison. Think on me
That am with Phoebus' amorous pinches black
And wrinkled deep in time? Broad-fronted Caesar,
When thou wast here above the ground, I was
A morsel for a monarch; and great Pompey
Would stand and make his eyes grow in my brow;
There would he anchor his aspect, and die
With looking on his life.

Antony agrees to marry Octavia, Caesar's sister, in order to help settle the differences between himself and Caesar. Meanwhile, Enobarbus entertains two of Caesar's followers with his stories about Cleopatra.

Act II, ii (lines 200–50)

ENOBARBUS I will tell you.
The barge she sat in, like a burnished throne,
Burned on the water; the poop was beaten gold;
Purple the sails, and so perfumed that
The winds were love-sick with them; the oars were silver,
Which to the tune of flutes kept stroke, and made
The water which they beat to follow faster,
As amorous of their strokes. For her own person,
It beggared all description: she did lie
In her pavilion, cloth-of-gold of tissue,
O'erpicturing that Venus where we see
The fancy outwork nature. On each side her
Stood pretty dimpled boys, like smiling cupids,
With divers-coloured fans, whose wind did seem
To glow the delicate cheeks which they did cool,
And what they undid did.

AGRIPPA O, rare for Antony!

ENOBARBUS Her gentlewomen, like the Nereides,
So many mermaids, tended her i'th' eyes,
And made their bends adornings. At the helm
A seeming mermaid steers. The silken tackle
Swell with the touches of those flower-soft hands
That yarely frame the office. From the barge
A strange invisible perfume hits the sense
Of the adjacent wharfs. The city cast
Her people out upon her, and Antony,
Enthroned i'th' market-place, did sit alone,
Whistling to th'air, which, but for vacancy,
Had gone to gaze on Cleopatra, too,
And made a gap in nature.

AGRIPPA Rare Egyptian!

ENOBARBUS Upon her landing, Antony sent to her;
Invited her to supper. She replied
It should be better he became her guest,
Which she entreated. Our courteous Antony,
Whom ne'er the word of 'No' woman heard speak,
Being barbered ten times o'er, goes to the feast,
And, for his ordinary, pays his heart
For what his eyes eat only.

AGRIPPA Royal wench!
She made great Caesar lay his sword to bed.
He ploughed her, and she cropped.

ENOBARBUS I saw her once
Hop forty paces through the public street
And, having lost her breath, she spoke and panted,
That she did make defect perfection,
And, breathless, pour breath forth.

MAECENAS Now Antony must leave her utterly.

ENOBARBUS Never! He will not.
Age cannot wither her, nor custom stale
Her infinite variety. Other women cloy
The appetite they feed, but she makes hungry
Where most she satisfies; for vilest things
Become themselves in her, that the holy priests
Bless her when she is riggish.

*The animosity between Antony and Caesar has not been resolved by
Antony's marriage to Octavia. Caesar has increased his power and
raised an army. Antony has sent Octavia to Caesar to mediate
between them while he also raises an army, and while she travels to
Rome he returns to Egypt without her knowledge. There, without
consulting Caesar, he bestows new honours and powers upon
Cleopatra and others. Caesar pursues Antony who ill-advisedly
resolves to fight him at sea. When Cleopatra's ships flee, Antony
follows. Afterwards, Antony is mortified and he turns on Cleopatra.*

Act III, xiii (lines 110–27)

ANTONY You were half blasted ere I knew you. Ha?
Have I my pillow left unpressed in Rome,
Forborne the getting of a lawful race,
And by a gem of women, to be abused
By one that looks on feeders?

CLEOPATRA Good my lord –

ANTONY You have been a boggler ever.
But when we in our viciousness grow hard –
O, misery on't! – the wise gods seel our eyes,
In our own filth drop our clear judgments, make us
Adore our errors, laugh at's while we strut
To our confusion.

CLEOPATRA O, is't come to this?

ANTONY I found you as a morsel, cold upon
Dead Caesar's trencher – nay, you were a fragment
Of Gnaeus Pompey's, besides what hotter hours,
Unregistered in vulgar fame, you have
Luxuriously picked out. For I am sure,
Though you can guess what temperance should be,
You know not what it is.

Alone with his servant Eros, Antony prepares to kill himself.

Act IV, xiv (lines 2–22)

ANTONY Sometime we see a cloud that's dragonish,
A vapour sometime like a bear or lion,
A towered-citadel, a pendent rock,
A forked mountain, or blue promontory
With trees upon't that nod unto the world
And mock our eyes with air. Thou hast seen these signs?
They are black vesper's pageants.

EROS Ay, my lord.

ANTONY That which is now a horse, even with a thought
The rack dislimns and makes it indistinct
As water is in water.

EROS It does, my lord.

ANTONY My good knave Eros, now thy captain is
Even such a body. Here I am Antony,
Yet cannot hold this visible shape, my knave.
I made these wars for Egypt, and the Queen –
Whose heart I thought I had, for she had mine,
Which, whilst it was mine, had annexed unto't
A million more, now lost – she, Eros, has
Packed cards with Caesar, and false-played my glory
Unto an enemy's triumph.
Nay, weep not, gentle Eros. There is left us
Ourselves to end ourselves.

Cleopatra witnesses Antony's death.

Act IV, xvi (lines 61–70)

CLEOPATRA Noblest of men, woo't die?
Hast thou no care of me? Shall I abide
In this dull world, which in thy absence is
No better than a sty? O see, my women,
The crown o'th' earth doth melt. My lord!
[*Antony dies.*]
O withered is the garland of the war,
The soldier's pole is fallen; young boys and girls
Are level now with men, the odds is gone
And there is nothing left remarkable
Beneath the visiting moon.

*Cleopatra, now in the hands of Caesar's followers Proculeius and
Dolabella, recalls the dead Antony.*

Act V, ii (lines 75–99)

CLEOPATRA I dreamt there was an emperor Antony.
O, such another sleep, that I might see
But such another man!

DOLABELLA If it might please ye –

CLEOPATRA His face was as the heavens, and therein stuck
A sun and moon which kept their course and lighted
The little O, the earth.

DOLABELLA Most sovereign creature –

CLEOPATRA His legs bestrid the ocean; his reared arm
Crested the world; his voice was propertied
As all the tuned spheres, and that to friends;
But when he meant to quail and shake the orb,
He was as rattling thunder. For his bounty,
There was no winter in't; an autumn it was
That grew the more by reaping. His delights
Were dolphin-like: they showed his back above
The element they lived in. In his livery
Walked crowns and crownets; realms and islands were
As plates dropped from his pocket.

DOLABELLA Cleopatra –

CLEOPATRA Think you there was or might be such a man
As this I dreamt of?

DOLABELLA Gentle madam, no.

CLEOPATRA You lie up to the hearing of the gods!
But if there be nor ever were one such,
It's past the size of dreaming. Nature wants stuff
To vie strange forms with fancy; yet t'imagine
An Antony were nature's piece 'gainst fancy,
Condemning shadows quite.

Dolabella has told Cleopatra of Caesar's plans to display her and her children in Rome. Cleopatra resolves to thwart these plans by killing herself.

Act V, ii (lines 206–31)

CLEOPATRA Now, Iras, what think'st thou?
Thou an Egyptian puppet shall be shown
In Rome as well as I. Mechanic slaves
With greasy aprons, rules and hammers shall
Uplift us to the view. In their thick breaths,
Rank of gross diet, shall we be enclouded
And forced to drink their vapour.

IRAS The gods forbid!

CLEOPATRA Nay, 'tis most certain, Iras. Saucy lictors
Will catch at us like strumpets, and scald rhymers
Ballad us out o'tune. The quick comedians
Extemporally will stage us and present
Our Alexandrian revels; Antony
Shall be brought drunken forth; and I shall see
Some squeaking Cleopatra boy my greatness
I'th' posture of a whore.

IRAS O the good gods!

CLEOPATRA Nay, that's certain.

IRAS I'll never see't, for I am sure my nails
Are stronger than mine eyes!

CLEOPATRA Why, that's the way
To fool their preparation and to conquer
Their most absurd intents.

Enter CHARMIAN.

Now, Charmian!
Show me, my women, like a queen. Go fetch
My best attires. I am again for Cydnus
To meet Mark Antony. Sirrah Iras, go.
Now, noble Charmian, we'll dispatch indeed,
And when thou hast done this chare, I'll give thee leave
To play till doomsday. Bring our crown and all.

CORIOLANUS

Written and first performed in 1608

Caius Martius is an outstanding Roman general, who is given the title of Coriolanus after the forthcoming battle against the Volscians, led by Aufidius. He is openly contemptuous of the citizens of Rome and the powers that have been given to them by the state.

Act I, i (lines 162–87)

MARTIUS What's the matter, you dissentious rogues
That, rubbing the poor itch of your opinion,
Make yourselves scabs?

1 CITIZEN We have ever your good word.

MARTIUS He that will give good words to thee, will flatter
Beneath abhorring. What would you have, you curs,
That like nor peace nor war? The one affrights you,
The other makes you proud. He that trusts to you,
Where he should find you lions, finds you hares;
Where foxes, geese: you are no surer, no,
Than is the coal of fire upon the ice,
Or hailstone in the sun. Your virtue is,
To make him worthy whose offence subdues him,
And curse that justice did it. Who deserves greatness,
Deserves your hate; and your affections are
A sick man's appetite, who desires most that
Which would increase his evil. He that depends
Upon your favours, swims with fins of lead,
And hews down oaks with rushes. Hang ye! Trust ye?
With every minute you do change a mind,
And call him noble that was now your hate,
Him vile that was your garland. What's the matter,
That in these several places of the city,
You cry against the noble Senate, who
(Under the gods) keep you in awe, which else
Would feed on one another? What's their seeking?

Junius Brutus, one of the tribunes of the people, describes to his fellow tribune Sicinius the popular reception of Caius Martius following his conquest of Corioles.

Act II, i (lines 205–21)

BRUTUS All tongues speak of him, and the bleared sights
Are spectacled to see him. Your prattling nurse
Into a rapture lets her baby cry
While she chats him. The kitchen malkin pins
Her richest lockram 'bout her reechy neck,
Clamb'ring the walls to eye him; stalls, bulks, windows,
Are smother'd up, leads fill'd and ridges hors'd
With variable complexions, all agreeing
In earnestness to see him. Seld-shown flamens
Do press among the popular throngs, and puff
To win a vulgar station. Our veil'd dames
Commit the war of white and damask in
Their nicely gauded cheeks, to th'wanton spoil
Of Phoebus' burning kisses. Such a pother,
As if that whatsoever god who leads him
Were slily crept into his human powers,
And gave him graceful posture.

*As a result of his bravery in battle the Roman Senate wishes to make
Coriolanus a consul. Coriolanus has now to speak to the citizens of
Rome who have the power to endorse or refuse this wish.
Reluctantly he does so.*

Act II, iii (lines 111–35)

CORIOLANUS Most sweet voices!
Better it is to die, better to starve,
Than crave the hire which first we do deserve.
Why in this wolvish toge should I stand here,
To beg of Hob and Dick that does appear
Their needless vouches? Custom calls me to't.
What custom wills, in all things should we do't,
The dust on antique time would lie unswept
And mountainous error be too highly heap'd
For truth to o'erpeer. Rather than fool it so,
Let the high office and the honour go
To one that would do thus. I am half through,
The one part suffer'd, the other will I do.

Enter three CITIZENS *more.*

Here come moe voices.
Your voices! For your voices I have fought,
Watch'd for your voices; for your voices, bear
Of wounds two dozen odd; battles thrice six
I have seen and heard of; for your voices have
Done many things, some less, some more: your voices!
Indeed I would be consul.

6 CITIZEN He has done nobly, and cannot go without any honest
man's voice.

7 CITIZEN Therefore let him be consul. The gods give him joy,
and make him good friend to the people!

ALL Amen, amen. God save thee, noble consul!

The Roman citizens have been swayed by the tribunes to withdraw their support for Coriolanus. In the Senate, goaded by the tribunes' accusations, Coriolanus attacks the powers bestowed on the people, and refuses to restrain his comments. He is accused of treason and there is civil unrest. When confronted by the tribunes, Coriolanus is again unable to restrain his anger and he is banished. He turns his back on them in contempt.

Act III, iii (lines 120–35)

CORIOLANUS You common cry of curs! whose breath I hate
As reek o'th' rotten fens, whose loves I prize
As the dead carcasses of unburied men
That do corrupt my air: I banish you!
And here remain with your uncertainty!
Let every feeble rumour shake your hearts!
Your enemies, with nodding of their plumes,
Fan you into despair! Have the power still
To banish your defenders, till at length
Your ignorance – which finds not till it feels,
Making but reservation of yourselves,
Still your own foes – deliver you as most
Abated captives to some nation
That won you without blows! Despising
For you the city, thus I turn my back.
There is a world elsewhere!

Histories

— ◇ —

KING HENRY VI, PART 1

Written and first performed 1590–2

Following the death of Henry V of the house of Lancaster, his infant son has ascended the throne. In France the English are being defeated by the French; in England there is political discord. The houses of Lancaster and York have rival claims to the throne, which flair up into open hostility.

Act II, iv (lines 25–55)

PLANTAGENET Since you are tongue-tied and so loath to speak,
In dumb significants proclaim your thoughts:
Let him that is a true-born gentleman
And stands upon the honour of his birth,
If he suppose that I have pleaded truth,
From off this brier pluck a white rose with me.

SOMERSET Let him that is no coward nor no flatterer,
But dare maintain the party of the truth,
Pluck a red rose from off this thorn with me.

WARWICK I love no colours; and without all colour
Of base insinuating flattery
I pluck this white rose with Plantagenet.

SUFFOLK I pluck this red rose with young Somerset,
And say withal I think he held the right.

VERNON Stay, lords and gentlemen, and pluck no more
Till you conclude that he upon whose side
The fewest roses from the tree are cropp'd
Shall yield the other in the right opinion.

SOMERSET Good Master Vernon, it is well objected:
If I have fewest, I subscribe in silence.

PLANTAGENET And I.

VERNON Then for the truth and plainness of the case,
I pluck this pale and maiden blossom here,
Giving my verdict on the white rose side.

SOMERSET Prick not your finger as you pluck it off,
Lest, bleeding, you do paint the white rose red,
And fall on my side so against your will.

VERNON If I, my lord, for my opinion bleed,
Opinion shall be surgeon to my hurt
And keep me on the side where still I am.

SOMERSET Well, well, come on: who else?

KING HENRY VI, PART 3

Written and first performed 1590–2

The Duke of York has been captured by Henry VI's army, led by Queen Margaret, and mocked with the death of his young son Edmund, Earl of Rutland. In his grief he rebukes Queen Margaret for her cruelty.

Act I, iv (lines 137–46)

YORK O tiger's heart wrapp'd in a woman's hide!
How could'st thou drain the life-blood of the child
To bid the father wipe his eyes withal,
And yet be seen to bear a woman's face?
Women are soft, mild, pitiful, and flexible;
Thou stern, indurate, flinty, rough, remorseless.
Bid'st thou me rage? Why, now thou hast thy wish
Would'st have me weep? Why, now thou hast thy will.
For raging wind blows up incessant showers,
And when the rage allays, the rain begins.

Edward, the eldest son of the Duke of York, has been crowned king.
At court his brother Richard muses on his own ambition to be king.

Act III, ii (lines 182–95)

RICHARD Why, I can smile, and murder whiles I smile,
And cry 'Content!' to that that grieves my heart,
And wet my cheeks with artificial tears,
And frame my face to all occasions.
I'll drown more sailors than the Mermaid shall;
I'll slay more gazers than the basilisk;
I'll play the orator as well as Nestor,
Deceive more slily than Ulysses could,
And, like a Sinon, take another Troy.
I can add colours to the chameleon,
Change shapes with Proteus for advantages,
And set the murderous Machiavel to school.
Can I do this, and cannot get a crown?
Tut! were it further off, I'll pluck it down.

KING RICHARD II

Written and first performed about 1595

Henry Bolingbroke, Duke of Hereford, and Thomas Mowbray have accused each other of treachery. In judgment King Richard banishes them both from England. Bolingbroke discusses his banishment with his father John of Gaunt, Duke of Lancaster.

Act I, iii (lines 275–305)

GAUNT All places that the eye of heaven visits
Are to a wise man ports and happy havens.
Teach thy necessity to reason thus –
There is no virtue like necessity.
Think not the king did banish thee,
But thou the king. Woe doth the heavier sit
Where it perceives it is but faintly borne.
Go, say I sent thee forth to purchase honour,
And not the king exil'd thee; or suppose
Devouring pestilence hangs in our air,
And thou art flying to a fresher clime.
Look what thy soul holds dear, imagine it
To lie that way thou goest, not whence thou com'st.
Suppose the singing birds musicians,
The grass whereon thou tread'st the presence strew'd,
The flowers fair ladies, and thy steps no more
Than a delightful measure or a dance;
For gnarling sorrow hath less power to bite
The man that mocks at it and sets it light.

BOLINGBROKE O, who can hold a fire in his hand
By thinking on the frosty Caucasus?
Or cloy the hungry edge of appetite
By bare imagination of a feast?
Or wallow naked in December snow
By thinking on fantastic summer's heat?
O no, the apprehension of the good

Gives but the greater feeling to the worse.
Fell sorrow's tooth doth never rankle more
Than when he bites, but lanceth not the sore.

GAUNT Come, come, my son, I'll bring thee on thy way,
Had I thy youth and cause, I would not stay.

On his deathbed John of Gaunt surveys the state of the kingdom under Richard II's rule.

Act II, i (lines 31–68)

GAUNT Methinks I am a prophet new inspir'd,
And thus expiring do foretell of him:
His rash fierce blaze of riot cannot last.
For violent fires soon burn out themselves;
Small showers last long, but sudden storms are short;
He tires betimes that spurs too fast betimes;
With eager feeding food doth choke the feeder;
Light vanity, insatiate cormorant,
Consuming means, soon preys upon itself.
This royal throne of kings, this scept'red isle,
This earth of majesty, this seat of Mars,
This other Eden, demi-paradise,
This fortress built by Nature for herself
Against infection and the hand of war,
This happy breed of men, this little world,
This precious stone set in the silver sea,
Which serves it in the office of a wall,
Or as a moat defensive to a house,
Against the envy of less happier lands;
This blessed plot, this earth, this realm, this England,
This nurse, this teeming womb of royal kings,
Fear'd by their breed, and famous by their birth,
Renowned for their deeds as far from home,
For Christian service and true chivalry,
As is the sepulchre in stubborn Jewry
Of the world's ransom, blessed Mary's son;
This land of such dear souls, this dear dear land,
Dear for her reputation through the world,
Is now leas'd out – I die pronouncing it –
Like to a tenement or pelting farm.
England, bound in with the triumphant sea,
Whose rocky shore beats back the envious siege
Of wat'ry Neptune, is now bound in with shame,

With inky blots and rotten parchment bonds;
That England, that was wont to conquer others,
Hath made a shameful conquest of itself.
Ah, would the scandal vanish with my life,
How happy then were my ensuing death!

During negotiations between Richard II and Lord Northumberland,
representing Henry Bolingbroke, now Duke of Lancaster, Richard
contemplates his powerlessness.

Act III, iii (lines 143–86)

RICHARD What must the king do now? Must he submit?
The king shall do it. Must he be depos'd?
The king shall be contented. Must he lose
The name of king? a God's name, let it go.
I'll give my jewels for a set of beads;
My gorgeous palace for a hermitage;
My gay apparel for an almsman's gown;
My figur'd goblets for a dish of wood;
My sceptre for a palmer's walking staff;
My subjects for a pair of carved saints,
And my large kingdom for a little grave,
A little little grave, an obscure grave,
Or I'll be buried in the king's highway,
Some way of common trade, where subjects' feet
May hourly trample on their sovereign's head;
For on my heart they tread now whilst I live:
And buried once, why not upon my head?
Aumerle, thou weep'st (my tender-hearted cousin!),
We'll make foul weather with despised tears;
Our sighs and they shall lodge the summer corn,
And make a dearth in this revolting land.
Or shall we play the wantons with our woes,
And make some pretty match with shedding tears?
As thus to drop them still upon one place,
Till they have fretted us a pair of graves
Within the earth, and therein laid – there lies
Two kinsmen digg'd their graves with weeping eyes!
Would not this ill do well? Well, well, I see
I talk but idly, and you laugh at me.
Most mighty prince, my Lord Northumberland,
What says King Bolingbroke? Will his Majesty

Give Richard leave to live till Richard die?
You make a leg, and Bolingbroke says 'ay'.

NORTHUMBERLAND My lord, in the base court he doth attend
To speak with you; may it please you to come down?

RICHARD Down, down I come, like glist'ring Phaeton,
Wanting the manage of unruly jades.
In the base court? Base court, where kings grow base,
To come at traitors' calls, and do them grace!
In the base court? Come down? Down, court! down, king!
For night-owls shriek where mounting larks should sing.

Exeunt from above.

BOLINGBROKE What says his Majesty?

NORTHUMBERLAND Sorrow and grief of heart
Makes him speak fondly like a frantic man;
Yet he is come.

Richard II abdicates in favour of Henry Bolingbroke.

Act IV, i (lines 200–22)

BOLINGBROKE Are you contented to resign the crown?

RICHARD Ay, no; no, ay; for I must nothing be.
Therefore no 'no', for I resign to thee.
Now, mark me how I will undo myself.
I give this heavy weight from off my head,
And this unwieldy sceptre from my hand,
The pride of kingly sway from out my heart;
With mine own tears I wash away my balm,
With mine own hands I give away my crown,
With mine own tongue deny my sacred state,
With mine own breath release all duteous oaths;
All pomp and majesty I do forswear;
My manors, rents, revenues, I forgo;
My acts, decrees, and statutes I deny.
God pardon all oaths that are broke to me,
God keep all vows unbroke are made to thee!
Make me, that nothing have, with nothing griev'd,
And thou with all pleas'd, that hast all achiev'd.
Long may'st thou live in Richard's seat to sit,
And soon lie Richard in an earthy pit.
God save King Henry, unking'd Richard says,
And send him many years of sunshine days!
What more remains?

KING RICHARD III

Written and first performed 1597

Richard, Duke of Gloucester, reveals his ambitions.

Act I, i (lines 1–41)

RICHARD Now is the winter of our discontent
Made glorious summer by this son of York;
And all the clouds that lour'd upon our House
In the deep bosom of the ocean buried.
Now are our brows bound with victorious wreaths,
Our bruised arms hung up for monuments,
Our stern alarums chang'd to merry meetings,
Our dreadful marches to delightful measures.
Grim-visag'd War hath smooth'd his wrinkled front:
And now, instead of mounting barbed steeds
To fright the souls of fearful adversaries,
He capers nimbly in a lady's chamber,
To the lascivious pleasing of a lute.
But I, that am not shap'd for sportive tricks,
Nor made to court an amorous looking-glass;
I, that am rudely stamp'd, and want love's majesty
To strut before a wanton ambling nymph:
I, that am curtail'd of this fair proportion,
Cheated of feature by dissembling Nature,
Deform'd, unfinish'd, sent before my time
Into this breathing world scarce half made up –
And that so lamely and unfashionable
That dogs bark at me, as I halt by them –
Why, I, in this weak piping time of peace,
Have no delight to pass away the time,
Unless to spy my shadow in the sun,
And descant on mine own deformity.
And therefore, since I cannot prove a lover
To entertain these fair well-spoken days,
I am determined to prove a villain,

And hate the idle pleasures of these days.
Plots have I laid, inductions dangerous,
By drunken prophecies, libels, and dreams,
To set my brother Clarence and the King
In deadly hate, the one against the other:
And if King Edward be as true and just
As I am subtle, false, and treacherous,
This day should Clarence closely be mew'd up
About a prophecy, which says that 'G'
Of Edward's heirs the murderer shall be –
Dive, thoughts, down to my soul: here Clarence comes.

Richard marvels at his success in winning the hand of Lady Anne, widow of Edward, Prince of Wales, whom he killed less than three months before.

Act I, ii (lines 232–68)

RICHARD Was ever woman in this humour woo'd?
Was ever woman in this humour won?
I'll have her, but I will not keep her long.
What, I that kill'd her husband and his father:
To take her in her heart's extremest hate,
With curses in her mouth, tears in her eyes,
The bleeding witness of her hatred by,
Having God, her conscience, and these bars against me –
And I, no friends to back my suit at all
But the plain devil and dissembling looks –
And yet to win her, all the world to nothing!
Ha!
Hath she forgot already that brave prince,
Edward, her lord, whom I, some three months since,
Stabb'd in my angry mood at Tewkesbury?
A sweeter and a lovelier gentleman,
Fram'd in the prodigality of Nature,
Young, valiant, wise, and no doubt right royal,
The spacious world cannot again afford.
And will she yet debase her eyes on me,
That cropp'd the golden prime of this sweet prince,
And made her widow to a woeful bed?
On me, whose all not equals Edward's moiety?
On me, that halts and am misshapen thus?
My dukedom to a beggarly denier,
I do mistake my person all this while!
Upon my life, she finds – although I cannot –
Myself to be a marvellous proper man.
I'll be at charges for a looking-glass,
And entertain a score or two of tailors
To study fashions to adorn my body:
Since I am crept in favour with myself,

I will maintain it with some little cost.
But first I'll turn yon fellow in his grave,
And then return, lamenting, to my love.
Shine out, fair sun, till I have bought a glass,
That I may see my shadows as I pass.

Richard, now King, is challenged for the crown by the Earl of Richmond, later Henry VII. They meet in battle at Bosworth. When overwhelmed by Richmond's troops Richard refuses to withdraw.

Act V, iv (lines 7–13)

KING RICHARD A horse! A horse! My kingdom for a horse!

CATESBY Withdraw, my lord; I'll help you to a horse.

KING RICHARD Slave! I have set my life upon a cast,
And I will stand the hazard of the die.
I think there be six Richmonds in the field:
Five have I slain today instead of him.
A horse! A horse! My kingdom for a horse!

KING HENRY IV, PART 1

....

Written and first performed about 1597

In a tavern in Eastcheap, London, Hal (the Prince of Wales) and Falstaff engage in their customary banter.

Act I, ii (lines 1–12)

FALSTAFF Now, Hal, what time of day is it, lad?

PRINCE Thou art so fat-witted with drinking of old sack, and unbuttoning thee after supper, and sleeping upon benches after noon, that thou hast forgotten to demand that truly which thou wouldst truly know. What a devil hast thou to do with the time of the day? Unless hours were cups of sack, and minutes capons, and clocks the tongues of bawds, and dials the signs of leaping-houses, and the blessed sun himself a fair hot wench in flame-coloured taffeta, I see no reason why thou shouldst be so superfluous to demand the time of the day.

When he is alone in the tavern, Hal reveals his reasons for appearing to be dissolute.

Act I, ii (lines 190–212)

PRINCE I know you all, and will awhile uphold
The unyok'd humour of your idleness.
Yet herein will I imitate the sun,
Who doth permit the base contagious clouds
To smother up his beauty from the world,
That, when he please again to be himself,
Being wanted he may be more wonder'd at
By breaking through the foul and ugly mists
Of vapours that did seem to strangle him.
If all the year were playing holidays,
To sport would be as tedious as to work;
But when they seldom come, they wish'd-for come,
And nothing pleaseth but rare accidents:
So when this loose behaviour I throw off,
And pay the debt I never promised,
By how much better than my word I am,
By so much shall I falsify men's hopes;
And like bright metal on a sullen ground,
My reformation, glitt'ring o'er my fault,
Shall show more goodly, and attract more eyes
Than that which hath no foil to set it off.
I'll so offend, to make offence a skill,
Redeeming time when men think least I will.

Henry Percy (Hotspur) has clashed with the King after refusing to hand over his prisoners taken in battle against the Scots. He contemplates rebellion.

Act I, iii (lines 195–206)

HOTSPUR O, the blood more stirs
To rouse a lion than to start a hare!

NORTHUMBERLAND Imagination of some great exploit
Drives him beyond the bounds of patience.

HOTSPUR By heaven, methinks it were an easy leap
To pluck bright honour from the pale-fac'd moon,
Or dive into the bottom of the deep,
Where fathom-line could never touch the ground,
And pluck up drowned honour by the locks,
So he that doth redeem her thence might wear
Without corrival all her dignities:
But out upon this half-fac'd fellowship!

In the tavern in Eastcheap Hal and Falstaff play out an imaginary conversation between the King and Hal.

Act II, iv (lines 454–75)

FALSTAFF I would your Grace would take me with you: whom means your Grace?

PRINCE That villainous abominable misleader of youth, Falstaff, that old white-bearded Satan.

FALSTAFF My lord, the man I know.

PRINCE I know thou dost.

FALSTAFF But to say I know more harm in him than in myself were to say more than I know. That he is old, the more the pity, his white hairs do witness it, but that he is, saving your reverence, a whoremaster, that I utterly deny. If sack and sugar be a fault, God help the wicked! If to be old and merry be a sin, then many an old host that I know is damned: if to be fat be to be hated, then Pharaoh's lean kine are to be loved. No, my good lord; banish Peto, banish Bardolph, banish Poins – but for sweet Jack Falstaff, kind Jack Falstaff, true Jack Falstaff, valiant Jack Falstaff, and therefore more valiant, being as he is old Jack Falstaff, banish not him thy Harry's company, banish not him thy Harry's company, banish plump Jack, and banish all the world.

PRINCE I do, I will.

KING HENRY IV, PART 2

Written and first performed in 1598

In Henry IV, Part 1 *the Chief Justice sought out Falstaff in connection with the robbery carried out at Gad's Hill. In Part 2 he rebukes Falstaff for failing to meet him when ordered to, and for leading Hal, the Prince of Wales, astray. Falstaff refuses to show remorse.*

Act I, ii (lines 178–201)

CHIEF JUSTICE Do you set down your name in the scroll of youth, that are written down old with all the characters of age? Have you not a moist eye, a dry hand, a yellow cheek, a white beard, a decreasing leg, an increasing belly? Is not your voice broken, your wind short, your chin double, your wit single, and every part about you blasted with antiquity? And will you yet call yourself young? Fie, fie, fie, Sir John!

FALSTAFF My lord, I was born about three of the clock in the afternoon, with a white head, and something a round belly. For my voice, I have lost it with hallooing, and singing of anthems. To approve my youth further, I will not: the truth is, I am only old in judgment and understanding; and he that will caper with me for a thousand marks, let him lend me the money, and have at him! For the box of the ear that the Prince gave you, he gave it like a rude prince, and you took it like a sensible lord. I have checked him for it, and the young lion repents – [*aside*] marry, not in ashes and sackcloth, but in new silk and old sack.

CHIEF JUSTICE Well, God send the Prince a better companion!

FALSTAFF God send the companion a better prince! I cannot rid my hands of him.

King Henry IV's health is declining. In his nightgown he considers the sleeplessness which accompanies his kingship.

Act III, i (lines 4–31)

KING How many thousand of my poorest subjects
Are at this hour asleep! O sleep, O gentle sleep,
Nature's soft nurse, how have I frighted thee,
That thou no more wilt weigh my eyelids down,
And steep my senses in forgetfulness?
Why rather, sleep, liest thou in smoky cribs,
Upon uneasy pallets stretching thee,
And husht with buzzing night-flies to thy slumber,
Than in the perfum'd chambers of the great,
Under the canopies of costly state,
And lull'd with sound of sweetest melody?
O thou dull god, why li'st thou with the vile
In loathsome beds, and leav'st the kingly couch
A watch-case, or a common 'larum-bell?
Wilt thou upon the high and giddy mast
Seal up the ship-boy's eyes, and rock his brains
In cradle of the rude imperious surge,
And in the visitation of the winds,
Who take the ruffian billows by the top,
Curling their monstrous heads, and hanging them
With deafing clamour in the slippery clouds,
That with the hurly death itself awakes?
Canst thou, O partial sleep, give thy repose
To the wet sea-boy in an hour so rude,
And in the calmest and most stillest night,
With all appliances and means to boot,
Deny it to a King? Then happy low, lie down!
Uneasy lies the head that wears a crown.

The Earl of Warwick and the King discuss the state of the kingdom. They recognise that the abdication and murder of Richard II has resulted in long-term conflict.

Act III, i (lines 80–94)

WARWICK There is a history in all men's lives
Figuring the nature of the times deceas'd;
The which observ'd, a man may prophesy,
With a near aim, of the main chance of things
As yet not come to life, who in their seeds
And weak beginnings lie intreasured.
Such things become the hatch and brood of time;
And by the necessary form of this
King Richard might create a perfect guess
That great Northumberland, then false to him,
Would of that seed grow to a greater falseness,
Which should not find a ground to root upon
Unless on you.

KING Are these things then necessities?
Then let us meet them like necessities;
And that same word even now cries out on us.

The King counsels Hal as his successor.

Act IV, v (lines 183–215)

KING God knows, my son,
By what by-paths and indirect crook'd ways
I met this crown, and I myself know well
How troublesome it sat upon my head.
To thee it shall descend with better quiet,
Better opinion, better confirmation,
For all the soil of the achievement goes
With me into the earth. It seem'd in me
But as an honour snatch'd with boist'rous hand,
And I had many living to upbraid
My gain of it by their assistances,
Which daily grew to quarrel and to bloodshed,
Wounding supposed peace. All these bold fears
Thou seest with peril I have answered;
For all my reign hath been but as a scene
Acting that argument. And now my death
Changes the mood, for what in me was purchas'd
Falls upon thee in a more fairer sort;
So thou the garland wear'st successively.
Yet though thou stand'st more sure than I could do,
Thou art not firm enough, since griefs are green;
And all my friends, which thou must make thy friends,
Have but their stings and teeth newly ta'en out;
By whose fell working I was first advanc'd,
And by whose power I well might lodge a fear
To be again displac'd; which to avoid,
I cut them off, and had a purpose now
To lead out many to the Holy Land,
Lest rest and lying still might make them look
Too near unto my state. Therefore, my Harry,
Be it thy course to busy giddy minds
With foreign quarrels, that action hence borne out
May waste the memory of the former days.

Hal, now King Henry V, dashes Falstaff's hopes of advancement.

Act V, v (lines 46–70)

FALSTAFF My King! My Jove! I speak to thee, my heart!

KING I know thee not, old man. Fall to thy prayers.
How ill white hairs becomes a fool and jester!
I have long dreamt of such a kind of man,
So surfeit-swell'd, so old, and so profane;
But being awak'd I do despise my dream.
Make less thy body hence, and more thy grace;
Leave gormandizing; know the grave doth gape
For thee thrice wider than for other men.
Reply not to me with a fool-born jest;
Presume not that I am the thing I was;
For God doth know, so shall the world perceive,
That I have turn'd away my former self;
So will I those that kept me company.
When thou dost hear I am as I have been,
Approach me, and thou shalt be as thou wast,
The tutor and the feeder of my riots.
Till then I banish thee, on pain of death,
As I have done the rest of my misleaders,
Not to come near our person by ten mile.
For competence of life I will allow you,
That lack of means enforce you not to evils;
And as we hear you do reform yourselves,
We will, according to your strengths and qualities,
Give you advancement.

KING HENRY V

....

Written and first performed about 1599

In the Prologue the Chorus asks the audience to use their
imagination to make up for the limitations of the theatre.

Prologue (lines 10–23)

CHORUS On this unworthy scaffold to bring forth
So great an object. Can this cockpit hold
The vasty fields of France? Or may we cram
Within this wooden O the very casques
That did affright the air at Agincourt?
O pardon, since a crooked figure may
Attest in little place a million,
And let us, ciphers to this great account,
On your imaginary forces work.
Suppose within the girdle of these walls
Are now confined two mighty monarchies,
Whose high upreared and abutting fronts
The perilous narrow ocean parts asunder.
Piece out our imperfections with your thoughts.

King Henry V is discussing with the Archbishop of Canterbury how
he may both take an army to France to reclaim his titles and also
safeguard England from a Scottish invasion. The Archbishop
describes a kingdom that emulates the order perceived to exist in
the natural world.

Act I, ii (lines 183–214)

CANTERBURY Therefore doth heaven divide
The state of man in diverse functions,
Setting endeavour in continual motion,
To which is fixed, as an aim or butt,
Obedience. For so work the honey-bees,
Creatures that by a rule in nature teach
The act of order to a peopled kingdom.
They have a king and officers of sorts,
Where some like magistrates correct at home,
Others like merchants venture trade abroad,
Others like soldiers, armed in their stings,
Make boot upon the summer's velvet buds,
Which pillage they with merry march bring home
To the tent-royal of their emperor,
Who busied in his majesty surveys
The singing masons building roofs of gold,
The civil citizens kneading up the honey,
The poor mechanic porters crowding in
Their heavy burdens at his narrow gate,
The sad-eyed justice, with his surly hum,
Delivering o'er to executors pale
The lazy yawning drone. I this infer,
That many things having full reference
To one consent may work contrariously,
As many arrows loosed several ways
Come to one mark,
As many several ways meet in one town,
As many fresh streams meet in one salt sea,
As many lines close in the dial's centre.
So may a thousand actions once afoot
End in one purpose and be all well borne
Without defeat.

Mistress Quickly, the hostess of a tavern in Eastcheap, describes the death of Falstaff.

Act II, iii (lines 4–25)

PISTOL Bardolph, be blithe. Nym, rouse thy vaunting veins.
Boy, bristle thy courage up;
For Falstaff he is dead, and we must earn therefore.

BARDOLPH Would I were with him, wheresome'er he is, either in heaven or in hell!

HOSTESS Nay, sure, he's not in hell; he's in Arthur's bosom, if ever man went to Arthur's bosom. 'A made a finer end, and went away an it had been any christom child. 'A parted even just between twelve and one, even at the turning o'th' tide. For after I saw him fumble with the sheets and play wi'th' flowers, and smile upon his fingers' ends, I knew there was but one way; for his nose was as sharp as a pen, and 'a babbled of green fields. 'How now, Sir John?' quoth I, 'what, man! be o' good cheer.' So 'a cried out 'God, God, God!' three or four times. Now I, to comfort him, bid him 'a should not think of God; I hoped there was no need to trouble himself with any such thoughts yet. So 'a bade me lay more clothes on his feet. I put my hand into the bed and felt them, and they were as cold as any stone. Then I felt to his knees, and so up'ard and up'ard, and all was as cold as any stone.

In France before the siege of Harfleur, Henry V rouses his troops.

Act III, i (lines 1–34)

KING Once more unto the breach, dear friends, once more,
Or close the wall up with our English dead.
In peace there's nothing so becomes a man
As modest stillness and humility;
But when the blast of war blows in our ears,
Then imitate the action of the tiger:
Stiffen the sinews, conjure up the blood,
Disguise fair nature with hard-favoured rage.
Then lend the eye a terrible aspect;
Let it pry through the portage of the head
Like the brass cannon; let the brow o'erwhelm it
As fearfully as doth a galled rock
O'erhang and jutty his confounded base,
Swilled with the wild and wasteful ocean.
Now set the teeth and stretch the nostril wide,
Hold hard the breath and bend up every spirit
To his full height. On, on, you noble English,
Whose blood is fet from fathers of war-proof,
Fathers that like so many Alexanders
Have in these parts from morn till even fought,
And sheathed their swords for lack of argument.
Dishonour not your mothers; now attest
That those whom you called fathers did beget you.
Be copy now to men of grosser blood
And teach them how to war. And you, good yeomen,
Whose limbs were made in England, show us here
The mettle of your pasture; let us swear
That you are worth your breeding – which I doubt not,
For there is none of you so mean and base
That hath not noble lustre in your eyes.
I see you stand like greyhounds in the slips,
Straining upon the start. The game's afoot.
Follow your spirit, and upon this charge
Cry 'God for Harry! England and Saint George!'

The Chorus describes the English army on the eve of the Battle of Agincourt. The soldiers are cold and few in number.

Act IV, Chorus (lines 15–47)

CHORUS The country cocks do crow, the clocks do toll,
And the third hour of drowsy morning name.
Proud of their numbers and secure in soul,
The confident and over-lusty French
Do the low-rated English play at dice,
And chide the cripple tardy-gaited night
Who like a foul and ugly witch doth limp
So tediously away. The poor condemned English,
Like sacrifices, by their watchful fires
Sit patiently and inly ruminate
The morning's danger; and their gesture sad,
Investing lank-lean cheeks and war-torn coats,
Presenteth them unto the gazing moon
So many horrid ghosts. O now, who will behold
The royal captain of this ruined band
Walking from watch to watch, from tent to tent,
Let him cry 'Praise and glory on his head!'
For forth he goes and visits all his host,
Bids them good morrow with a modest smile,
And calls them brothers, friends and countrymen.
Upon his royal face there is no note
How dread an army hath enrounded him,
Nor doth he dedicate one jot of colour
Unto the weary and all-watched night,
But freshly looks and overbears attaint
With cheerful semblance and sweet majesty,
That every wretch, pining and pale before,
Beholding him plucks comfort from his looks.
A largess universal, like the sun,
His liberal eye doth give to every one,
Thawing cold fear, that mean and gentle all
Behold, as may unworthiness define,
A little touch of Harry in the night.

The King rallies his troops as they prepare to face the overwhelming power of the French army.

Act IV, iii (lines 40–67)

KING This day is called the feast of Crispian.
He that outlives this day and comes safe home
Will stand a-tiptoe when this day is named
And rouse him at the name of Crispian.
He that shall see this day and live old age
Will yearly on the vigil feast his neighbours,
And say 'Tomorrow is Saint Crispian,'
Then will he strip his sleeve and show his scars,
And say 'These wounds I had on Crispin's Day.'
Old men forget; yet all shall be forgot
But he'll remember, with advantages,
What fears he did that day. Then shall our names,
Familiar in his mouth as household words,
Harry the King, Bedford and Exeter,
Warwick and Talbot, Salisbury and Gloucester,
Be in their flowing cups freshly remembered.
This story shall the good man teach his son,
And Crispin Crispian shall ne'er go by
From this day to the ending of the world
But we in it shall be remembered,
We few, we happy few, we band of brothers.
For he today that sheds his blood with me
Shall be my brother; be he ne'er so vile,
This day shall gentle his condition.
And gentlemen in England now abed
Shall think themselves accursed they were not here,
And hold their manhoods cheap whiles any speaks
That fought with us upon Saint Crispin's day.

SONNETS

SONNET 18

Shall I compare thee to a summer's day?
Thou art more lovely and more temperate:
Rough winds do shake the darling buds of May,
And summer's lease hath all too short a date:
Sometime too hot the eye of heaven shines,
And often is his gold complexion dimmed;
And every fair from fair sometime declines,
By chance, or nature's changing course, untrimmed:
But thy eternal summer shall not fade,
Nor lose possession of that fair thou ow'st,
Nor shall death brag thou wander'st in his shade
When in eternal lines to time thou grow'st:
   So long as men can breathe or eyes can see,
   So long lives this, and this gives life to thee.

SONNET 29

When in disgrace with fortune and men's eyes
I all alone beweep my outcast state,
And trouble deaf heav'n with my bootless cries,
And look upon myself, and curse my fate,
Wishing me like to one more rich in hope,
Featured like him, like him with friends possessed,
Desiring this man's art and that man's scope,
With what I most enjoy contented least;
Yet in these thoughts myself almost despising,
Haply I think on thee, and then my state,
Like to the lark at break of day arising,
From sullen earth sings hymns at heaven's gate;
  For thy sweet love remembered such wealth brings
  That then I scorn to change my state with kings.

SONNET 33

Full many a glorious morning have I seen
Flatter the mountain tops with sovereign eye,
Kissing with golden face the meadows green,
Gilding pale streams with heavenly alchemy;
Anon permit the basest clouds to ride
With ugly rack on his celestial face,
And from the forlorn world his visage hide,
Stealing unseen to west with this disgrace:
Even so my sun one early morn did shine
With all triumphant splendour on my brow;
But out alack, he was but one hour mine,
The region cloud hath masked him from me now.
  Yet him for this, my love no whit disdaineth:
  Suns of the world may stain, when heaven's sun staineth.

SONNET 34

Why didst thou promise such a beauteous day
And make me travail forth without my cloak,
To let base clouds o'ertake me in my way,
Hiding thy brav'ry in their rotten smoke?
'Tis not enough that through the cloud thou break,
To dry the rain on my storm-beaten face,
For no man well of such a salve can speak
That heals the wound and cures not the disgrace;
Nor can thy shame give physic to my grief;
Though thou repent, yet I have still the loss;
Th'offender's sorrow lends but weak relief
To him that bears the strong offence's loss.
  Ah, but those tears are pearl which thy love sheds,
  And they are rich, and ransom all ill deeds.

SONNET 55

Not marble, nor the gilded monuments
Of princes, shall outlive this powerful rhyme;
But you shall shine more bright in these contents
Than unswept stone, besmeared with sluttish time.
When wasteful war shall statues overturn
And broils root out the work of masonry,
Nor Mars his sword, nor war's quick fire, shall burn
The living record of your memory:
'Gainst death, and all oblivious enmity,
Shall you pace forth; your praise shall still find room
Even in the eyes of all posterity
That wear this world out to the ending doom.
  So till the judgment that yourself arise,
   You live in this, and dwell in lovers' eyes.

SONNET 60

Like as the waves make towards the pebbled shore,
So do our minutes hasten to their end,
Each changing place with that which goes before,
In sequent toil all forwards do contend.
Nativity, once in the main of light,
Crawls to maturity; wherewith being crowned
Crooked eclipses 'gainst his glory fight,
And time, that gave, doth now his gift confound.
Time doth transfix the flourish set on youth,
And delves the parallels in beauty's brow;
Feeds on the rarities of nature's truth,
And nothing stands but for his scythe to mow.
  And yet to times in hope my verse shall stand,
  Praising thy worth, despite his cruel hand.

SONNET 64

When I have seen by time's fell hand defaced
The rich proud cost of outworn buried age;
When sometime lofty towers I see down razed,
And brass eternal slave to mortal rage;
When I have seen the hungry ocean gain
Advantage on the kingdom of the shore,
And the firm soil win of the wat'ry main,
Increasing store with loss, and loss with store;
When I have seen such interchange of state,
Or state itself confounded, to decay,
Ruin hath taught me thus to ruminate:
That time will come and take my love away.
  This thought is as a death, which cannot choose
  But weep to have that which it fears to lose.

SONNET 73

That time of year thou mayst in me behold,
When yellow leaves, or none, or few do hang
Upon those boughs which shake against the cold,
Bare ruined choirs where late the sweet birds sang;
In me thou seest the twilight of such day
As after sunset fadeth in the west,
Which by and by black night doth take away,
Death's second self that seals up all in rest;
In me thou seest the glowing of such fire
That on the ashes of his youth doth lie,
As the deathbed, whereon it must expire,
Consumed with that which it was nourished by;
  This thou perceiv'st, which makes thy love more strong,
  To love that well, which thou must leave ere long.

SONNET 87

Farewell, thou art too dear for my possessing,
And like enough thou knowst thy estimate;
The charter of thy worth gives thee releasing;
My bonds in thee are all determinate.
For how do I hold thee but by thy granting,
And for that riches where is my deserving?
The cause of this fair gift in me is wanting,
And so my patent back again is swerving.
Thyself thou gav'st, thy own worth then not knowing,
Or me, to whom thou gav'st it, else mistaking;
So thy great gift upon misprision growing
Comes home again, on better judgment making.
  Thus have I had thee as a dream doth flatter,
  In sleep a king, but waking no such matter.

SONNET 97

How like a winter hath my absence been
From thee, the pleasure of the fleeting year!
What freezings have I felt, what dark days seen,
What old December's bareness everywhere!
And yet this time removed was summer's time,
The teeming autumn big with rich increase
Bearing the wanton burden of the prime,
Like widowed wombs after their lords' decease:
Yet this abundant issue seemed to me
But hope of orphans, and unfathered fruit;
For summer and his pleasures wait on thee,
And thou away, the very birds are mute;
　　Or if they sing, 'tis with so dull a cheer
　　That leaves look pale, dreading the winter's near.

SONNET 104

To me, fair friend, you never can be old;
For as you were when first your eye I eyed,
Such seems your beauty still: three winters cold
Have from the forests shook three summers' pride;
Three beauteous springs to yellow autumn turned
In process of the seasons have I seen;
Three April perfumes in three hot Junes burned,
Since first I saw you fresh, which yet art green.
Ah, yet doth beauty, like a dial hand,
Steal from his figure, and no pace perceived;
So your sweet hue, which methinks still doth stand,
Hath motion, and mine eye may be deceived;
  For fear of which, hear this, thou age unbred,
  Ere you were born was beauty's summer dead.

SONNET 106

When in the chronicle of wasted time
I see descriptions of the fairest wights,
And beauty making beautiful old rhyme,
In praise of ladies dead, and lovely knights;
Then in the blazon of sweet beauties best,
Of hand, of foot, of lip, of eye, of brow,
I see their antique pen would have expressed
Even such a beauty as you master now:
So all their praises are but prophecies
Of this our time, all you prefiguring;
And for they looked but with divining eyes
They had not skill enough your worth to sing;
   For we which now behold these present days
   Have eyes to wonder, but lack tongues to praise.

SONNET 107

Not mine own fears, nor the prophetic soul
Of the wide world, dreaming on things to come,
Can yet the lease of my true love control,
Supposed as forfeit to a confined doom.
The mortal moon hath her eclipse endured,
And the sad augurs mock their own presage;
Uncertainties now crown themselves assured,
And peace proclaims olives of endless age.
Now with the drops of this most balmy time
My love looks fresh, and death to me subscribes,
Since 'spite of him I'll live in this poor rhyme,
While he insults o'er dull and speechless tribes;
   And thou in this shalt find thy monument,
    When tyrants' crests and tombs of brass are spent.

SONNET 116

Let me not to the marriage of true minds
Admit impediments; love is not love
Which alters when it alteration finds,
Or bends with the remover to remove.
O no, it is an ever-fixed mark,
That looks on tempests and is never shaken;
It is the star to every wand'ring bark,
Whose worth's unknown, although his height be taken.
Love's not Time's fool, though rosy lips and cheeks
Within his bending sickle's compass come;
Love alters not with his brief hours and weeks,
But bears it out even to the edge of doom.
   If this be error and upon me proved,
   I never writ, nor no man ever loved.

SONNET 130

....

My mistress' eyes are nothing like the sun;
Coral is far more red than her lips' red;
If snow be white, why then her breasts are dun;
If hairs be wires, black wires grow on her head;
I have seen roses damasked, red and white,
But no such roses see I in her cheeks;
And in some perfumes is there more delight
Than in the breath that from my mistress reeks.
I love to hear her speak, yet well I know
That music hath a far more pleasing sound;
I grant I never saw a goddess go;
My mistress when she walks treads on the ground.
  And yet, by heaven, I think my love as rare
  As any she belied with false compare.

INDEX OF FIRST LINES

— ◇ —

A

B

C

D

F

INDEX OF CHARACTERS

— ◇ —

INDEX OF THEMES AND REFERENCES

— ◇ —

215